A Man of Many
Names

To Mum and Aunty B
– faithful first readers.

A Man of Many Names

Olaudah Equiano

Emily J. Maurits

CF4•K

10 9 8 7 6 5 4 3 2 1

Copyright © 2022 Emily J. Maurits
Paperback ISBN: 978-1-5271-0876-9
Ebook ISBN: 978-1-5271-0956-8

Published by Christian Focus Publications,
Geanies House, Fearn, Tain, Ross-shire,
IV20 1TW, Scotland, U.K.
www.christianfocus.com;
email: info@christianfocus.com

Cover design by Daniel van Straaten
Cover illustration by Daniel van Straaten
Printed and bound by Nørhaven, Denmark

Contents

The Fortunate One

Olaudah Equiano wiggled, and tugged at his mother's blue robe. 'Is it time, yet?'

'Soon.' She curled an arm around his shoulder, pulling him close. Olaudah Equiano breathed in the scent of her perfume. The mixture of powdered wood and palm oil smelt rich and heavy, and some days he liked to sit beside her quietly and simply breathe it in – but not today.

'Now?' he asked, using her arm to pull himself up on the tips of his toes. The golden bangles on her wrist jangled, but before she could reply, Olaudah Equiano caught sight of his older brother. 'Here they come!' he cried, as a group of blue-clothed men came out of the plastered wattle house, his elder brother in front. Olaudah Equiano's father was with them, and Equiano released his grip on his mother's arm.

'Remember, do not interrupt,' his mother said, holding him back before he could run up to the men. 'This is a very special moment for your brother, and your father is a very special man.'

Olaudah Equiano fidgeted. I know that, he thought. His father was one of the ruling elders in his village. He was respected by all, and this meant he had a lot of power. It also meant that today Olaudah's older brother would receive a special mark on his forehead. Yet knowing wasn't the same as seeing, and so Olaudah pulled at his mother's hand. He'd never watched a marking before and wanted a good view.

Olaudah Equiano's mother allowed herself to be led forward a few steps, and then shook her arm free. 'Go on,' she said. 'One day you will fight for our people and have many children and many slaves. You do not need me, I will stay here.'

But Olaudah Equiano felt like he needed his mother very much! He watched as the bearded priests, who usually kept quite separate from the rest of the clan, joined the group of men and boys. Perhaps, Olaudah decided, the view from where his mother stood was good enough.

Then his father spotted him. 'Olaudah Equiano! Come here, and watch this great event.' As his older brother sat down on the carved wooden chair normally reserved for visitors, Olaudah Equiano edged forward until he had joined the outer ring of men. They made way for him. 'It is good,' said one of the priests quietly, 'for us to have a fortunate one here.'

A fortunate one. *They were talking about him.* Olaudah Equiano swallowed, but before he could think about the meaning of his name for long, the priest pulled out a knife and approached his brother.

Olaudah saw his brother's hands clench around the edge of the chair as the priest drew the knife across his brother's forehead. For a moment there was a long pale streak and then the priest pulled at the skin until it came down to his brother's eyebrows, and began rubbing a hand over the wound. Olaudah watched carefully, but his brother's eyes were closed and his lips were pressed together. He did not make a sound. I hope I'm that brave when it's my turn, thought Olaudah. Behind his brother, Olaudah's father stood proudly, his own mark criss-crossing over his forehead. It had healed long ago into a distinguished web-like design.

Equiano touched his own smooth forehead and grinned. One day he would be just like his brother and father. But first, there were New Year celebrations to enjoy! As the priests and elders began to disperse, Equiano scampered over to his mother.

'Wait! Olaudah Equiano!' Olaudah turned back to see a bearded priest standing alone in front of the house. 'Come back.'

Olaudah trotted over to the old man, twisting his hands. Although the priests were healers, they could also perform magic to discover who had committed a crime. Olaudah's mind whirred. He couldn't *remember* doing anything wrong …

'Fortunate One.'

'Priest,' he said respectfully.

'You are called Fortunate One, but there is a way to increase your fortune.'

'Yes, priest?'

'I have heard that there are two snakes which come sometimes into your night-house and lay nearby as you and your mother sleep.'

'Yes, priest,' said Olaudah Equiano. The long grey snakes, as thick as his father's leg, were harmless and he knew it would be very wrong to hurt them. Yet Olaudah still shivered at the sight of them coiled in the moonlight. Everyone knew the grey snakes were signs that something bad was about to happen … and when they appeared, Olaudah was always reminded of the other meanings of his name. The meanings which were less talked about.

'We must place them in a large pan and put them elsewhere,' said the bearded priest, 'but first I want you to touch them, Olaudah. When a fortunate one, like yourself, holds these snakes, bad things will not happen to you. Rather, you will become more fortunate than ever.'

'Yes, priest.' said Olaudah, breathing out. 'Shall we do it now?'

'Yes,' nodded the old man. 'New Year's Day is the right time to collect good omens.'

* * *

'Rattle – rattle – rattle!'

As the sun set on the first day of the year, the sound of rattles filled every part of the West African village of Essaka. Olaudah shook his own rattle hard, welcoming in the new year as a gift from the great god. He shouted and held out his hands to heaven for a blessing. All around him men, women and children, priests and elders, stretched out their hands in the mauve twilight, shouting and rattling their musical instruments.

One year was over, a new one had begun.

This would be a good year, Olaudah was certain of it. Although he had shivered earlier as he had held the grey snakes, he was grateful for their good fortune, and had felt very special as he placed them in the priest's pan. Now as he watched, the elders and heads of family were beginning to bring their animals over to the priests. Burnt offerings and sacrifices were made often, at many special occasions, but particularly at the beginning of the year. His stomach rumbled and Olaudah looked forward to eating the smoky meat with the rest of his family afterward, some offerings with bitter herbs, others with yams or corn. Was that his sister, at the shadowy edge of the crowd? He began to push his way towards her, but just then, a loud voice called out: 'Fetch the fortunate ones!'

It was time for the Presenting.

'Olaudah? There you are.' Hands on his shoulders, Olaudah's mother guided him to an elder. The old man placed his hands on Olaudah's head. 'Olaudah Equiano. Fortunate one with a loud-voice, well-spoken, who will experience favour and vicissitude,' he said, reciting the prophecy which the priests had made at Equiano's birth. Olaudah's people, the Igbo, believed that every child had an inescapable destiny which was often reflected in the names they were given at birth.

As Olaudah and the other 'lucky' children were presented and handed around the crowd, he couldn't help but wonder about the last part of his name. Everyone who touched him hoped to gain some of his good fortune, and Olaudah was sure that good fortune would follow him just as the priests had prophesied. Yet what about 'vicissitude'? Vicissitude meant unwelcome changes might also come …

When the time for the feast arrived, Olaudah was set down on his feet. The partying crowd had begun to retreat to their individual houses, stomachs rumbling, mouths thirsty for palm wine. Olaudah looked around for his mother. *Was that her on the road?* He made his way towards the track, yawning as his feet made contact with the beaten dirt. Where was she?

Then, all of a sudden, part of the road moved! Olaudah froze, throat tightening. *Is it an evil spirit?* He looked down, and saw it wasn't the road which was moving, it was a dust-coloured snake! Olaudah held his breath, squinting in the near darkness. He hoped it was one of the harmless, grey ones he'd helped remove earlier, but with a squirm in his chest, he noticed it was much thinner and darker. It was a different snake, a poisonous one.

Held tight by fear, Olaudah could do nothing but watch as the snake wove its way between his ankles, bringing death closer and closer with every arc-like movement. His heart knocked against his chest. *Will it bite me now? Or now? Or now?*

To Olaudah's surprise, the snake's shifting body passed through his legs without stopping, writhing across the road and into the night. The moment it disappeared, he fell to the ground, knees giving way. *I'm safe, I'm safe —*

'Olaudah Equiano!' The priest stood by the side of the track, staring at him with wide eyes. 'It didn't bite you!' The man hurried over and helped him up, wiping the dust from his body and shaking his head in disbelief. 'You truly are fortunate! This is a remarkable omen!'

Olaudah, his fear retreating, gave a wobbly smile. Deep in his heart he felt a gush of peace. Surely this meant that the second part of his destiny was wrong. Only fortune would come to him. There would be no unwelcome changes, no unhappiness.

* * *

As the battle raged below, Olaudah Equiano leaned back against the cool trunk of the ube tree and closed his eyes. At first it had all been very exciting. For days his village had been preparing for an attack, placing sharpened sticks dipped in poison at their doors each morning as they went out to work. Olaudah had followed the adults, trailing out to the vegetable fields with a thrilling sense of expectation, dreaming of the moment when the men and women would exchange their hoes for weapons.

Yet when the neighbouring chief arrived with an army, his mother had turned to him, sword in hand. 'Run! Hide!'

It was difficult to see who was who through the branches of the tree Olaudah Equiano had chosen, and Olaudah was bored. The shouts and clanging from the battlefield melded into background noise, which was in turn drowned out by the leaves rustling in the wind.

One day I'm going to fight in a battle like that, he thought, eyes still shut. I'm going to defend our village, just like my mother. One day I'm going to have an estate all of my own.

I'll have a sleeping house like father, for me and my male children. And another one for my wives, and another for my guests, and many for my slaves, and still more for the slaves of my slaves, he planned. All the buildings will be plastered with the cow-dung mixture used to keep away insects, and we will sleep soundly. Each day we'll all go out to work in the fields, and when we're not working I'll sit with my friends in my day-house and smoke pipes and eat stewed meat and plantains. My houses will be surrounded with a red-earth wall and a moat and we will be safe from kidnappers and dangerous animals.

Olaudah smiled. *It will be a fortunate life.*

'Olaudah! Olaudah!'

At the sound of his mother's voice, Olaudah almost fell out of the tree. *Did I fall asleep?* He rubbed his eyes and scrambled to the ground, landing at his mother's feet. 'Mother? We won?'

'We won.' Olaudah's mother smiled and wiped the sweat off her forehead. 'It is time to purify ourselves now, come along.'

As they completed the ceremonial washing which was required after battle, before eating, and at other special times, Olaudah craned his neck to try and spot the new faces. 'Did we capture many people, mother?'

'Many.'

'Do you think they'll all be redeemed? Will Father keep the ones who aren't?'

'Maybe,' his mother replied, splashing water up to her forearms. 'Although if we're to have any more slaves, we'll need to build more houses!'

Olaudah laughed, and having already washed, moved away. I will get my javelin, he thought, and the war-medals Mother made me, and then go find the other children. We can play battles all afternoon.

* * *

'Mother? Are you going out to see grandmother?'

'Yes,' said Olaudah's mother, cradling a bowl against her body. Behind her, Olaudah's father and his six siblings sat eating the evening meal. A short distance away their slaves sat in family groups, eating the same food. 'Wait here.'

'Please, I want to come with you!'

She sighed. 'Alright then. But you must not interrupt.'

'I won't!' Olaudah followed her out of the walled property and down the road. The sun was setting, streaking gold across the tops of the trees. There was a rustling and squawking as a flock of birds erupted into the now inky sky. Olaudah and his mother walked down a little rutted path, keeping an eye out for snakes and other creatures, until they reached a small thatched hut.

Grandmother's tomb. Olaudah swallowed. 'Mother?'

'Yes?'

'How do I know what the priests say about me will come true?' Olaudah asked.

Olaudah's mother moved past him and knelt down in front of the tomb. She placed the bowl of animal's blood, which she'd brought as an offering, in front of her.

'The priests speak the words of god, Olaudah. The creator of all, who lives in the sun, and neither eats nor drinks. He has planned out your days, my son, and knows when you will live or die. You are favoured and fortunate.'

And when the sun disappeared and the air around him became thick with insects and the sounds of his mother's wailing and the cries of night-time animals, Olaudah held onto those words. All through the night, while his mother grieved and cried out to the dead, Olaudah wrapped his trembling arms around his knees and repeated to himself: *You are favoured and fortunate. You are favoured and fortunate.*

He hoped it was enough to keep him safe.

Kidnapped!

'And where have these slaves come from?' Olaudah's father asked the traders.

'They're all criminals or prisoners of war,' the head trader replied, shifting a large empty sack from hand to hand. He and his fellow traders had come from the south west of Olaudah's village and wished to travel through their land. Their skin was redder than that of the people in Essaka, and Olaudah and his village called them Oye-Igbo, which means 'red men living at a distance.'

'Very well,' Olaudah's father said. 'Now, shall we do the usual trade – our perfumes, wood and salt for your gunpowder, beads and dried fish?'

The two men departed to talk business, and Olaudah shuffled his feet. He had already looked at all the interesting things for sale in the marketplace. 'Mother? Can I go and play now?'

His mother was watching the two men talking. 'Yes,' she said, but as Olaudah turned to go, she called out. 'Wait!'

'Yes, Mother?'

'Make sure you set a look-out before you start your games,' she said, tightening her blue robe. 'It's very important.'

'We will,' Olaudah promised.

* * *

Olaudah was again sitting high up in a tree, his legs dangling over nothingness. The sun was hot, even under the tree branches, and the shouts of the playing children sounded like the calling of far away birds.

I wonder whether god ever gets tired of watching people from his seat in the sun. Olaudah rubbed his eyes. When he reopened them he saw immediately that something had changed. He sat forward on his branch.

Below him a man was climbing over the wall of the neighbouring estate. The yard was full of children playing, and they had not noticed the kidnapper!

'Hey!' He shouted, scooting to the end of his branch and waving his arms, holding on tightly with his legs. 'Hey! Watch out!'

At last one of the children heard him and looked up. Olaudah pointed and waved, just as the man got to the top of the wall and dropped into the yard. Immediately the oldest children grabbed a nearby rope and threw it around the kidnapper.

Olaudah didn't stop to see what would happen next. He slid to the ground and, as soon as he felt dirt beneath his feet, ran to fetch the grown-ups.

* * *

'And that,' Olaudah Equiano said, 'is how I saved everyone from a kidnapper.'

His sister's eyes, which had been wide and staring during his story, narrowed. 'You didn't tie him up,' she protested. 'The other children did! All you did was raise the alarm.'

Olaudah crossed his arms. 'If I hadn't, they might not have seen him until it was too late.'

His sister laughed. 'What happened to him then?'

Olaudah shrugged. 'I don't know. Kidnapping is a big crime. Maybe he'll be made into a slave.'

'I'm going to ask Mother when she and the others get back,' his sister said, getting to her feet. Their property was empty. The other children, free and slave alike, were playing elsewhere, and the grown-ups were all working in the field. 'Do you want to play – Argghh!'

Olaudah turned, hunting in every direction for the snake.

There wasn't one. But in front of them stood a strange man and woman, a third man dropping down from the top of the beaten earth walls.

'Run!' Olaudah shouted, and grabbed his sister. As he did so, the kidnappers leapt forward and stuffed a piece of cloth into his mouth and seized his arms, twisting them behind him. Olaudah tried to shake them off, tried to move towards his sister, tried to scream, but they were too strong. He and his sister were hauled across the property, down the path, and into the nearby woods.

Please let the adults return early, thought Olaudah. Please let one of the other children see!

But nobody saw and nobody heard.

Under the cover of dark green foliage, the kidnappers tied their arms together with thick cord. Then they slung the two children onto their backs and began to walk.

Unable to cry out, unable to move, Olaudah had no choice but to bounce along the road in the kidnapper's arms until evening came. Just before the night stole his vision entirely, Olaudah saw a small house appear out of the darkness. Here they stopped, and the kidnappers dropped him to the ground and untied his hands.

Olaudah looked at his sister, shaking beside him, and looked at the three strong grown-ups sitting in front of the only door, eating and drinking. He reached out an arm to his sister, and, utterly exhausted, they fell asleep.

The next morning the kidnappers tied them up again and continued their journey through the woods. For hours they made their way over uneven ground and around knobbly trees. Then, without warning, the forest ended and a road began. A road which looked very familiar.

Perhaps, thought Olaudah, we will meet some people we know on the road and be rescued! Sure enough, after they'd walked for a little while, he spied some moving figures in the distance. His heart leapt.

'Help!' He yelled as loud as he could. 'Help!'

At once the kidnappers stopped and pushed the piece of cloth back into Olaudah's mouth, doing the same to his sister. Then they tied his arms tighter, and pushed him into a large sack. 'They won't even see you now,' said one of the kidnappers, 'we'll just carry the sacks right past them!'

And they did. Once again, nobody saw and nobody heard. Starving hungry, and beginning to realise that there was no hope of escape, Olaudah and his sister kept quiet until they stopped for the night and were untied.

'Here,' said one kidnapper, holding out some cold yam.

'No! I don't want it.' Olaudah was too upset and angry to eat. Instead, he and his sister wrapped their arms around each other and cried.

The next morning, they were separated.

'No, please!'

'Let us stay together!'

The kidnappers did not listen, and Olaudah Equiano watched as his sister was carried away. *Will I ever see her again?*

He cried for the rest of the journey, and ate only what the kidnappers forced into his mouth. Eventually they handed him to other traders, who handed him to other traders, and after many days of being passed from man to man like he was a piece of dried fish, Olaudah was given to a chief with two wives.

It was almost like returning home.

Although he was far away from his village, these people spoke his language and one of the wives comforted him and wiped away his tears.

'Is that a bellows?' Olaudah asked his new master, pointing at the leather bag and wooden handle which was attached to the stove.

'Yes,' the chief replied. 'I am a smith. I make all sorts of jewelry and I need you to push up and down on that wooden leaver, so the bellows will pump air into the fire, and keep it hot.'

After a month of pumping the bellows near the sooty fire and watching the smith turn his golden metal into bangles and bracelets, the family began to trust Olaudah and let him wander further from the house.

'Excuse me?' Olaudah hugged his empty water pot tight to his chest. He had volunteered to help the young women collect water in the cool of the evenings, because he had some very important questions to ask. 'What's in that direction?' He pointed towards the place where the sun rose.

'Another village,' a woman answered.

'And beyond that?'

'Another one.'

Home, thought Equiano. He filled his water pot and tried not to show his excitement. When he thought of his mother tears ran down his cheeks. But not for long now. Soon he would escape!

* * *

'There you are!' Olaudah emptied his pot of grain onto the ground in front of the speckled chickens. As he watched them eat, he tossed a pebble from hand to hand, lost in his dreams of escape. Any day now, he would sneak out. Surely it couldn't be too far to his village? He fiddled with the small rock and then, without thinking, threw it to the ground.

'Sqwark!' The rock hit one of the chickens, which staggered for a few steps and then fell over.

Olaudah stared at the bird, dread curdling in his stomach. What had he done? Quickly he dragged the limp chicken under a bush, hiding it beneath the thick green. Surely no one would notice.

But someone did notice. 'Oi! Boy! Come here.'

Olaudah approached the old slave woman, stomach clenched. 'Yes, Cook?'

'We're missing a chicken.' She peered at him. 'What have you done?'

Olaudah considered lying, but then he heard his mother's voice in his ear: *Never lie Olaudah. Lying is wrong.* He swallowed. 'I – I killed it.'

'What?' The old woman grabbed him by his shoulders and shook him. 'You killed it? You will pay for this! The master is out, but I'll get the mistress —'

Olaudah pulled away, and ran. He raced out of the wall-enclosed property and down the road. The time has come, he thought. I will escape today before I am found and punished. Then he stopped. It was morning. The roads would be busy; people were everywhere. Someone would certainly stop him. *But if I wait until nightfall …*

Olaudah stumbled to a stop, side aching, and flung himself into the thick bushes which surrounded the village. The leaves were so dense, surely no one would be able to see him.

For hours all Olaudah heard was his heart thumping in his ears and the voices of searchers. It sounded like the whole village was out looking for him.

'Have you found him?'

'No, not yet.'

Olaudah, muscles already aching from his cramped hiding place, curled himself tighter in the middle of the thicket. The speakers were directly in front of him! He held his breath. It would be evening soon, he just had to keep hidden until then …

'Do you think he's tried to return to his village?' One of the speakers asked. Olaudah could see the back of their legs through the leaves.

'I hope not,' the other replied. 'He'll never make it. It's days and days away, and the path is not marked out. He'll get lost in the woods or eaten by animals.'

Olaudah's heart sank. Until now he'd hoped that the journey had just seemed confusing because he'd been half-carried, half-dragged, weeping over the loss of his freedom and his sister. But now it sounded like getting home on his own really was impossible. *What should I do now?* he wondered. As the two men walked on, Olaudah burst into quiet tears.

Night fell. His legs trembling from hunger, his lips dry from thirst, Olaudah crept out of the thicket. Under the cover of darkness he made his way back to the open-walled kitchen and, exhausted, lay down in the cold ashes of the fireplace. He fell asleep.

'There you are!'

Olaudah woke, jumping away from the hands stretching towards him. It was the old slave woman – but instead of angry she looked astonished, and even relieved. 'Oh! You're alive! I thought you'd been eaten by animals!' She reached out again, and this time Olaudah let her pull him to his feet. 'Oh, you silly boy. I must go tell the master that you're safe! I'll tell him the chicken was an accident, do not worry.'

Olaudah sank back to the floor, shaking as he remembered the events of the previous day. While he was relieved not to be punished, he now knew that freedom was further away and would be harder to obtain than he'd thought. Still, he promised himself as he dusted grey ash from his skin, I'll get home. Next time anyone makes a journey, I'll ask to go along and then I'll run away. I just have to be patient.

But all the patience in the world could not help him a few weeks later when his master's only daughter died suddenly. Olaudah's master, the metalsmith, stopped making bracelets and bangles and, mad with grief, began to pace about the house. His family took turns sitting with him, afraid he would do something terrible in his sadness. When at last he recovered, he sold Olaudah to a passing trader.

As he was dragged away, Olaudah tried to understand why. *Do I remind my master of his lost daughter? Is my master in debt to the healers?* Either way, Olaudah was beginning to discover, if you were a slave you never really had a home.

Where would he be taken next?

In a World of Angry Spirits

Olaudah stumbled to a halt inside the small resting-house and stared. He rubbed his eyes and blinked, but the familiar figure did not disappear.

'Olaudah!' His sister launched herself out of the crowd of slaves and traders and flung her arms around his neck. 'Olaudah! Oh, I've missed you so much!'

Still unable to believe what was happening, Olaudah wrapped his arms around her warm body and squeezed. Tears dripped from his eyes down onto her shoulder, and he could feel his own neck getting damp from her tears too. He could not find any words, so he held her tight and hoped it was enough. *I love you so much.*

After a few moments, Olaudah heard a sniff. He looked up, only to see the traders in the hut looking almost as upset as his sister and him!

'Do you know each other?' asked one of them finally.

Olaudah nodded, not wanting to end the hug. 'She's my sister. My only sister.'

'Well,' said a trader, 'well.' He turned away. Another trader wiped his eyes. When it was time to sleep, the man who owned Olaudah spoke up. 'You can stay near your sister,' he said with a kind expression. 'We won't keep you away.'

'Thank you,' Olaudah whispered. All night he and his sister held hands across the chest of one of the traders, one on either side, grateful they were allowed to stay so close when usually men and women slept separately. Everything is going to be alright now, thought Olaudah, as he drifted off to sleep, his sister's fingers tangled with his. Everything is going to be alright.

But when morning came, the traders who owned Olaudah's sister set off, dragging her out of the door. 'Noo!' shouted Olaudah, but his owners held him back, and soon she was gone. *Where were they taking her? Would she be treated well? Will I ever see her again?*

His questions had no answers, and soon Olaudah himself was once again on the move.

* * *

'Here you go.' The man who was about to become Olaudah's second master counted out 172 little white cowry shells into the hand of the trader.

Olaudah looked around him. This new town, Tinmah, was more beautiful than any he'd seen so far in his travels through Africa. Sunlight glinted off a huge pond in the centre of the town, dazzling the eyes of the people washing. Behind the steady marketplace chatter, the voices of the many tiny streams flowing through the town whispered. *It's nice here, it's nice here*, they seemed to be saying. For the first time since his sister was taken away, Olaudah felt light-hearted. *At last, a place to call home.*

Olaudah's second master led him to a plastered, white-washed house similar to the ones in his own village. It was surrounded by shady trees. 'Here.'

'What is it?' Olaudah stared at the thing in his master's hand. It looked like half of a huge egg, except it was brown and furry! He took it carefully, and saw there was liquid inside.

'It's a coconut,' his new master said. 'You can drink the liquid and eat the white inside.'

Olaudah did – it was delicious! Shortly afterwards he tried sugar cane for the first time, and decided he liked his new home very much indeed!

* * *

'Olaudah?'

'Yes, sir?' Olaudah ran up to his master.

'Tell the cook we're going to have visitors this evening. My neighbour and her son are coming.'

'Yes, sir.' Olaudah did as he was told, and as the sun began to slide beneath the coconut trees, the visitors arrived.

As soon as they entered, Olaudah could tell that the lady, whom he later learned was a widow, was very wealthy. Her robes were woven of fine cloth and she had a great number of bangles and other jewellery. She smiled at Olaudah, turning to her son. 'Look! This boy is your age! Go play with him while I talk to our neighbour.'

By the end of the night, the rich lady had decided to buy Olaudah. She took him back with her that very night! Her estate was huge, with many houses and many slaves. The next morning, after he'd been washed and perfumed by the other slaves, Olaudah was led to his new mistress and her son.

Olaudah stood in the doorway and curled his toes into the beaten earth. His new mistress and her son were sitting and eating their morning meal.

'Ah, there you are!' the woman said, smiling. 'Come and sit down with us. Eat.'

Olaudah stared. While free men and slaves worked in the field together, and fought together, they never, ever ate together. He inched his way over to them and sat beside his young master, expecting to be told to go away, if not by his mistress, at least by her son. To his surprise the boy grinned, and pushed a bowl of vegetables towards him. 'You are the eldest,' he said, 'you must begin eating first.'

As the days passed, Olaudah began to think his mistress would adopt him into her family. He and his young master played bows and arrows together, ate together, and were even attended by the other slaves. Two months flew by, and each night as Olaudah lay down to rest, he remembered the meaning of his name, and smiled.

I really am fortunate.

* * *

'Argh –' Olaudah's shout was cut off by a hand across his mouth, and his arms were pressed behind him. He struggled, but was quickly dragged out of the night-house, his young master, his friend and almost-brother, still asleep.

What had made the rich lady decide to sell him? Olaudah had no time to find out. Once again he was on the road in the hands of slave traders. The difference between these new traders and the happy household he'd left behind was immense. Olaudah and all the men he'd met so far has been circumcised, but these traders were not. They also ate from iron pots, and had weapons he'd never seen before. When meal times came they did not wash their hands, and neither did they make sacrifices or offerings to the spirits. Instead, some of them filed their teeth into sharp points, and they decorated each other with scars very different to Olaudah's people.

'We can do it to you,' they said, when they saw him watching. 'Come here!'

'No, please!' Olaudah begged. He didn't want their ugly scars! He wanted his father's special forehead marking!

The men laughed, and travelled on. After many days Olaudah heard a strange sound. It was like the whisper of the streams in the village he'd left, but much louder. As they came around a bend in the road, Olaudah stopped and stared.

Lying in front of him was more water than he'd ever seen, more water than he'd ever imagined could exist. And what's more, there were people floating on it, sitting in things which looked a little bit like the half-coconut he'd eaten, but longer and thinner. When the traders brought him closer, Olaudah saw that the people had cups and bowls and food stores beside them – as if they lived on the water!

'Come on,' one of the traders grunted, 'get in the canoe, we're going on the river.'

Olaudah hesitated, but had no choice. He shook as the canoe shuddered beneath him, and held on tight when the men began to stir the water with sticks to make the canoe move faster. Soon, though, he was distracted from his fear by the sight of women diving off the canoes and swimming in the water. How brave they are! He thought. When night came, the traders brought the boats to land and built a fire, and some of them slept on the shore, while others slumbered in the canoes. Olaudah was very grateful he was allowed to sleep on dry ground.

For days and days the traders brought him over land and rivers until Olaudah began to think that he'd never stay in one place for more than a night ever again.

* * *

'What's that noise?' Olaudah asked one morning. It sounded like another big river, but different, more rhythmic. The air smelled funny too, a bit like the salt his mother made out of ashes.

'Ocean,' said one of the traders. They'd all been in a bad mood since the day before, as if they were nervous about something. Olaudah didn't speak again, until suddenly the land disappeared, and there was water in front of him as far as he could see. The blue of the water shook hands with the blue of the sky, and panic rose in Olaudah's throat.

'What's that?' he asked, pointing at what looked like a canoe, only a hundred times bigger and with white cloths hanging from towering sticks.

'The ship you're going on,' said the trader and, without warning, grabbed Olaudah and carried him down to the sand and onto the ship. Olaudah screamed, but the trader simply dumped him on the wooden planks and moved away. Olaudah scrambled to his feet and darted towards the planked walkway – right into the hands of an evil spirit.

'Arghh!' Olaudah shouted. The white-skinned spirit said something in a language he didn't understand, and then tossed him up into the air, pushing and pulling at his arms and legs, as if to make sure they worked. Then the spirit nodded to the African trader and pointed him towards another white spirit.

Olaudah turned slowly on the spot, spotting other Africans chained in rows on the deck, and a huge furnace letting off smoke in the centre of the ship, and came to one conclusion. The evil spirits were going to cook him up and eat him! Sweating, sick in his stomach with fear, Olaudah blinked, trying to see properly. Then everything went black.

* * *

He woke to see the African slave traders standing above him, clutching their bags of payment.

'There you are!' One said. Olaudah sat up, the world moving strangely around him. 'Don't worry, it's all going to be fine.'

Olaudah shook his head. 'No,' he managed to croak, and pointed at the ugly white spirits with their red faces and freely waving hair. 'I'm going to be eaten.'

The traders laughed. 'No, you're not!' they said. 'Look! They are bringing you a drink to make you feel better.'

Olaudah shrank back as a white spirit with yellow hair thrust a cup towards him. 'No!' he cried, certain it was poison.

One of the African traders took the cup. 'It's safe,' he said. 'Drink.'

Very thirsty, Olaudah drank, surprised to find there was only a mouthful or two of liquid in the cup. He was even more surprised to find it wasn't water! His throat burned as it went down, and he felt hotter and dizzier than before. He dropped back down on the deck, certain he was in a dream, or dying, or both.

What were they going to do to him?

* * *

It turned out that the ship was nothing like a canoe, and the white spirits really were nothing like the African traders. Olaudah and the other chained Africans were soon taken below deck. The smell of bodies and waste was horrible, and, already feeling sick from crying so hard, Olaudah thought he might throw up. He slumped against a wooden prop in the dimness of the hold, ignoring the men chained around him. I wish I'd thrown myself into the ocean, he thought. Anything is better than this!

'What's your name?'

Someone was speaking his language! Olaudah pulled himself upright and searched in the crowded darkness for the owner of the voice.

'Here!' A chain rattled. A man across from him tried to wave.

'Oh! What's going to happen to us? Please — tell me!' All Olaudah's terror came rushing back. 'How long before they eat us?'

'No, they're not going to eat us, child,' said the man, shaking his head. 'They will take us to their country to work for them.'

'To a spirit place?'

'They're not spirits. Just strange men.'

'They have a country? They don't live here, in this hollow place?' Olaudah swallowed.

'No, they come from far away.'

'Then how come, in all our land, we have not heard of them?'

'Because it is so very far.'

Olaudah had trouble imagining a country so far away, and one filled completely with white men! 'Do they have white women, like themselves? Where are they?'

'We think they left them behind.'

'How do we get there, then?' Olaudah asked.

'This big boat,' the man said. 'We don't know how it works, but they use cloth and ropes and wood to make it go, and when they want it to stop, they put a magic spell on the water.'

Olaudah shivered. Surely this old man was confused. How could these white men be anything but spirits? Soon they will return and eat me, he thought. I have to escape!

* * *

'Eat!'

Although he did not understand their strange language, Olaudah understood what the white spirits meant when they brought a bucket of boiled horse beans down below deck. He turned his face away, trying not to breathe through his nose as the smell of beans mingled with the scent of unwashed bodies and buckets of refuse.

'Oi, Michael! Eat!'

Olaudah shook his head. *Why do the white spirits give all the Africans new names? Why don't they call me Olaudah Equiano?* He wrapped his arms around himself and tried to sink into the shadows.

'Right. Take him above deck and beat him.'

White hands reached into the darkness and grabbed Olaudah by the arms.

'Noo!' he screamed. Where were they taking him?

He soon found out. A short while later, aching and humiliated, Olaudah was thrown back below deck.

'If you don't eat,' the old African said, 'they'll whip you every hour until you do.'

Olaudah stuck his chin out. 'I'm not hungry.'

Several hours later, he changed his mind.

* * *

For days the ship remained moored on the coast of Africa. It became more and more crowded below deck as new Africans were dragged aboard, until Olaudah Equiano could barely move. The smell got worse, and soon it was so unhealthy that the white spirits allowed Olaudah Equiano and the others to come up on deck each day to breathe fresh air.

Each time he was taken above deck, Equiano looked for a way to escape. But the white spirits watched him very closely, and had tacked nets around the side of the ship so no one could jump overboard. Escape seemed impossible.

'We're moving!'

Crammed below deck, his leg rubbing against someone's side, and his shoulder wedged beneath the head of another person, sweating from the heat and barely able to breathe, Equiano felt the movement of the ship beneath him. It was true! They really were leaving his country for the land of the white spirits. Despair curdled in his stomach. *Will I ever see my sister and my family again? Will I ever climb an ube tree again, or run down the track to my village?* He swallowed as tears tumbled down his cheeks, and everyone around him began to wail in the darkness.

Suffocating days below deck soon turned into dark, hopeless nights. Equiano forgot what silence was,

crammed tightly with hundreds of other frightened, sick
and dying slaves for weeks on end. He forgot what it was
like to be dry and comfortable. All he knew was damp
wood below him, aching bruises from being flung this
way and that with the swaying of the ship, and gnawing
hunger as the store of boiled beans and yams grew low.

It was only during his brief times above deck that
he remembered there was a world beyond the dark,
cramped hold. Equiano breathed in the fresh air after
four days straight below deck, and the world spun. He
gazed at the billowing clouds, and watched fish leap
out of the waves. He watched the white spirits as well,
trying to understand the magic which allowed them to
move such a huge ship through the water. Surely he was
in a world of wonder and enchantment.

'Look! They've caught fish!'

At the cry, Equiano looked over and saw that the
white spirits who weren't busy keeping an eye on him
were struggling with a net full of pale, slippery fish.
Hope rose in his throat. They would have fresh meat!
Perhaps the extra food would help slow the number of
deaths. For a week now, an illness had been spreading
from slave to slave, and every morning was saturated
with sobbing over those who died in the night.

He watched as the white spirits began to clean and
cook the fish. Soon the smell of frying fish filled the
air. Equiano swallowed, mouth filling with saliva. There
were far too many fish for the white spirits to eat by
themselves, and he waited impatiently.

At last the white spirits finished eating, licked their lips, and began gathering up the leftovers. Equiano and the other Africans on deck edged closer. A white spirit walked towards them, dragging a sack of fish – and then continued past them, and threw the uneaten fish over the side of the ship!

'No!' shouted a nearby slave. Equiano stared, stomach rumbling, unable to believe his eyes. How could anyone be so cruel?

'Please!' he called out, 'please, can we have some?'

The white men laughed and ignored them. That evening a few slaves tried to steal some leftover fish and were badly beaten.

And so the days stumbled by into months, months marked by death, disease and despair. What Equiano didn't know was that he and his fellow slaves were not the first ones to make this terrible voyage. In fact the journey from Africa to the West Indies and America was called the 'Middle Passage' and over 12.5 million Africans were taken there against their will, just like Equiano. Many didn't survive.

* * *

'Land!'

'Here at last!'

The white men sound so happy. Equiano shifted in the hold, trying to massage the cramps out of his legs. The next time he was brought above deck, he learned why. Instead of never-ending blue, he saw sand and trees, and a harbour full of boats just like theirs. There were houses too, but far taller than any he'd seen before, and white men riding on four-legged animals instead of walking. *Is this more magic?*

Their ocean journey had ended – but where was he?

Becoming Gustavus Vassa

'No, you won't be eaten,' said a black man in Equiano's language to the frightened slaves. The white sailors had brought him aboard the ship to explain to them what would happen next. 'You must stop wailing. You must eat. They want you to harvest sugar cane.'

This explanation didn't make Equiano feel much better when he and the others were herded off the ship, weak and stumbling, or when they were pushed into a crowded pen, surrounded by staring white men. A drum beat echoed over their heads, and then all at once, the gate of the pen was opened and the white men came rushing in! As the slaves shrunk back, the white men grabbed as many as they could lay their hands on, some even using handkerchiefs or ropes as a lasso. Brothers were torn apart, wailing and begging to be bought together, and Equiano watched with increasing loneliness when every one of his country men were led away.

'Looks like you're a reject, then.' said one of the white men to Equiano at the end of the day. The sugar season, where slaves were needed all over the island of Barbados to cut the sugar cane, was coming to a close. Even so, everyone on the ship was sold, except Equiano and a handful of others – all of them too thin and weak after the voyage to attract much attention.

'We'll have to feed you up on fat pork and try and sell you in Virginia,' said a slaver, pushing Equiano onto another ship.

* * *

Virginia, Equiano discovered, was a very lonely place. He was put to work weeding grass and picking up stones in a distant field on a large tobacco plantation. None of the other slaves he met spoke his language. To make matters worse, he was once again renamed.

'Oi! Jacob!' A slave waved his hand. The gesture meant, *follow me*. Leaving behind his pile of stones, Equiano followed the slave across the field and towards the house of their master. They entered through the door of what looked like a kitchen, and Olaudah stopped in shock. The black woman cooking over the stove had an iron cage fixed around her head. It kept her mouth closed so that she could not eat or drink, in case she stole any of the food she was preparing.

'Oi!' snapped the slave who was leading Equiano. He waved again, and Equiano walked on through the house. They went down a long hall and came into a cluttered room. There, on a couch, lay the white man who had bought Equiano off the slave ship. The other slave gave Equiano a fan, pointed to the resting white man, and pushed him inside.

Equiano gazed around with wide eyes, as he pushed the fan up and down. The room was filled with beautiful objects he'd never seen before. Then he heard a ticking sound. What was that? He searched for whoever was making the noise, still fanning cool air towards his sleeping master. At last he worked out it was coming from a round sort of face hanging from the chimney. Tick, tick, tick, it went. Equiano swallowed, and began to fan his master faster, certain the clock would tell on him if he didn't!

Then he spotted another face, peering down at him from a rectangle, wooden frame. *Is this more white man magic?* He remembered his visit to his grandmother's tomb. Perhaps white people kept their great men in boxes on the wall after they died? That would certainly make it easier to leave sacrifices.

Olaudah shivered, looking constantly from the staring eyes of the painting to the frowning face of the clock until at last his master woke and sent him out. He stumbled back into the field with relief, grateful to get far away from the white men's strange enchantments. Alone once more, the sun beating down on his bare back, Equiano sighed. *Could the prophecy about my name be wrong? There's nothing fortunate or favoured about my life now! I will never be a leader among my people, or make just judgements in a loud voice, like Father. Is all lost?*

* * *

'I'll buy him.' The man said to Equiano's master. 'Maybe I'll give him as a gift to my cousins in England.'

And that was how Equiano got his first ride on a horse! An old slave took him by horseback to the harbourside to join his new master, Michael Henry Pascal. Pascal was a lieutenant in the British Navy and wanted Equiano brought aboard his ship.

It was a much, much nicer place than the ship which had taken him from Africa. Equiano could scarcely believe it when the white sailors showed him some spare sails he could sleep on, and gave him plenty of food to eat.

'Please,' asked Equiano, trying to remember his few words of English, 'Where?'

'Oh!' the sailor laughed. 'Don't you worry, boy. We will take you back to Africa. Home!'

Home! Equiano was so happy he could have hugged the white sailor. *My new master is taking me home?* Equiano thought of all the strange wonders he had seen. What incredible stories he would be able to tell his family! Filled with joy he ran up to his new master as soon as he came aboard.

'Ah, there you are.' said Pascal. 'I've decided to name you Gustavus Vassa.'

Equiano frowned. He could understand enough English now to know what his new master was saying. But he didn't want to have his name changed again!

'Jacob,' he said, pointing at himself.

'No,' Pascal said. 'Gustavus Vassa. Now follow me.'

Equiano ignored him. *I won't answer him until he calls me Jacob.*

'Vassa! Come!'

Equiano did not come. Pascal, however, did come, and hit him over the head. And so it continued, until one day, head aching, Equiano gave in and began to answer to his new name.

'Gustavus Vassa' was the well-known name of a Swedish freedom fighter, which may sound like a strange name for a slave, but perhaps Pascal enjoyed the thought of owning a slave called 'freedom fighter' who had no freedom at all. In fact, many slave owners gave their slaves names of great men, calling them 'Caesar' or 'Augustus' as a joke.

'Hey, Vassa!'

Equiano turned – to see a white boy a few years older than him coming across the swaying deck.

'Hey! You're Pascal's slave, right? I'm Richard. I'm Pascal's servant. He's going to take me with him into the navy, and one day I might be an officer! I've never been at sea before. Perhaps we can be friends and help each other?'

Equiano was so surprised, he forgot to smile. *A white person wants to be friends?*

'We don't have to,' said Richard hurriedly, 'if you –'

'Friends, yes,' said Equiano, nodding and beginning to smile. 'Yes, please.'

At first the days flew by. It was so nice to have someone to answer his questions! Equiano's English grew better and better. Together he and Richard learnt about sea life. They huddled together at night when the waves grew very rough, and laughed in delight as they stood, shoulder by shoulder, watching the sunset spread across the sky. White men, understood Equiano for the first time, are not born mean, but can choose whether to be nice or cruel, just like Africans. Slowly he began to relax.

Then the food supplies grew low.

'The journey is taking longer than expected,' Richard told Equiano, having listened to the sailors' muttered conversation. 'They're worried we might run out.'

'Yes,' said Pascal, coming up. 'If our supplies grow any lower, we will have to kill and eat you!'

Equiano froze, all his worst dreams coming true.

'Yes,' laughed another sailor, 'You eat people in Africa, don't you, boy?'

Equiano shook his head. 'No! No, we don't. Please don't eat me!'

The men laughed, and every time someone commented on the lack of food, someone else would reply: 'It's alright, we can eat Vassa!'

Each time Equiano heard his name called, he trembled. Is this the day they will eat me? was his first thought. How awful, to be eaten just as I'm on my way home to Africa!

* * *

'Pull! Pull!' Muscles straining, the sailors pulled hard at the net, and hauled a huge, glistening shark out of the sea.

Equiano watched with relief. Now they would have fresh meat for a while, and he wouldn't have to be quite so afraid. A sailor took out his knife and sliced the top fin off the shark. Would they eat that bit first? Equiano wondered. Then, as he looked on, the finless shark was pushed back into the ocean, still flapping and twisting.

'No!' he cried. 'We eat!'

Pascal laughed. 'No, we'll eat you, if we get that desperate.'

Equiano shivered.

'But we'll eat Richard first, I think. He'll taste better.'

Richard! Equiano was filled with fear for his friend. From then on, he trembled, not only when his name was called, but when Richard's was called too. Sometimes he even crept after Richard and his master, and peered through slits in the door, to make sure Richard wasn't being eaten.

Then one night the sea was the roughest Equiano had ever seen it. The waves seemed to tower up to the heavens, and came crashing down with such force that one sailor was swept overboard.

'There he is!'

'Quick!'

Equiano held on tight to the wooden body of the ship as the waves grew and grew and the men shouted and ran about on deck. The terrible waves must mean that the ruler of the seas is very angry, he thought. They will need a sacrifice to make him happy. Who could be given to calm the storm?

My life is worth the least to the white men. They will sacrifice me. Terrified, Equiano did not manage to fall asleep for a single minute that entire night. It was only when morning came at last and the waves had settled without need for a sacrifice, that he began to relax. For now, he was safe.

* * *

'Splash!'

Equiano gazed over the side of the ship at the strange, dark fish swimming along beside them. *That is the biggest sea creature I've ever seen.* Then a fountain of water spurted out of a hole in its back, and he leapt back.

'Urgh.' Equiano wiped the whale's spray from his cheek, and as he did so, the waves flattened and the ship stopped moving. Equiano stared at the dark whale. It made the ship stop! He stumbled back on the slippery deck. *This must be the ruler of the sea. It's angry at us, because the white men never make any sacrifices,* he thought.

'Richard! Richard!' Equiano found his friend near the main mast, coiling up a long piece of rope. 'Will there be a —' he fumbled, not knowing the English word for 'sacrifice'. 'Will they give me to big fish to eat?'

Richard frowned, not understanding his friend, and not knowing that Equiano thought the whale was a sea god hungry for human sacrifice. 'Yes,' he said, 'A fish like that can swallow anyone.'

Equiano gulped. *This is it. I'll never see my family again now!*

'Oi! Vassa!'

Equiano ran up to Pascal, his master. 'Yes, sir?'

'What's this, you think the whale will eat you?' Pascal burst into laughter. 'Ha ha ha,' he turned to another sailor. 'Look at him trembling!'

Equiano licked his lips, eyes stinging.

'Ha ha ha,' laughed the sailor. 'What a good idea! We will feed him to the whale!'

All day Equiano waited, but no one came to grab him and finally in the evening, the whale swam away. He breathed out, sagging against the ship mast. *Safe once more.*

* * *

Yet it wasn't long before another problem appeared on the horizon.

'Land!'

Equiano and Richard raced to the side of the ship, where a sliver of land was visible — a very welcome sight after thirteen weeks at sea. Richard crowed with delight. 'England at last!'

England? Equiano stared at his sunburnt friend. 'Not Africa?' he asked in a very small voice, a sneaking suspicion beginning to rise in the back of his mind.

'Africa?' Richard turned and looked at him, shaggy eyebrows raised. 'Why would we be going to Africa? Our master lives in England, Vassa. He's taking us home with him.'

Equiano's shoulders slumped and he stared at the horizon until it went fuzzy, as if hoping that if he looked at it long enough, he could turn it into the African coast. *The sailors lied. I'm never going to see my family again.*

It was a long night.

When Equiano came out on deck the next morning, another surprise awaited him. The ship was covered in white powder!

'Sir! Sir!' Equiano ran to the ship's mate. 'Come see! Come see! In night someone put salt over ship!'

The sailor laughed. 'Go bring me some salt then, boy.'

Equiano raced back above deck, scooped up a handful of salt, and yelped. It was cold! Shivering he brought the cold salt back to the sailor.

'Now taste it.'

Equiano opened his mouth — and the salt dissolved on his tongue, leaving water behind! What's more, it didn't taste salty at all! The sailor bent over laughing.

'What is? What is?'

'It's called snow,' the sailor explained. 'Don't you have it in Africa?'

Equiano shook his head. 'What does it do? Who made it?'

'God did.'

'Who is God?'

The sailor scratched his head, as snow began to fall from the sky all around them, turning the rigging and ropes into huge white spiderwebs. Equiano pushed his cold hands beneath his armpits. 'God is ... well, he's a great man who lives in the heavens.'

Equiano frowned. Was this God the same as the African god who lived in the sun?

* * *

Before long, Equiano and Richard went ashore at Cornwall to attend church with their master.

'Why are we here?' Equiano whispered.

'To worship God,' Richard whispered back.

Equiano watched and listened as a man read from a book, and all the white people stood up to sing a song. This wasn't like any worship he had ever seen before.

'Why?' he asked.

'Because God made us and everything in the world.'

Equiano was very impressed. He soon noticed that not only did white people worship a very powerful God, but they also did not keep other white people as slaves. How happy they must be, Equiano thought. I want to find out more.

Another thing which surprised him was that Richard and his master wanted to spend their time ashore holding objects called books.

'What are you doing?'

'Reading.' Richard trailed his finger over the crinkly page. 'The book ... well, it tells us stories. Exciting stories about other people.'

Wow! Perhaps these books can answer all the questions I don't know how to ask. The next time Richard and Pascal went out, Equiano crept over to one of their books and picked it up.

Please, book,' he said, 'can you tell me how the world began?' He put his ear to the page, but heard nothing.

'Book, tell me more about the great God who makes snow.' But still the book was silent. Equiano put it back on the table, disappointed. Perhaps the books only speak to white men, he thought. But how am I supposed to find out more about this great God?

At War!

'War is coming soon.'

'Yes, against France. They want our colonies.'

'I've heard the French are gathering together a huge army. They mean to attack Canada, or perhaps England herself!'

Against the background of rumours of a coming war, Equiano, Pascal and Richard joined a naval ship. There were many other boys of Equiano's age on board, most training to be naval officers, like Richard. As his English improved, Equiano's fears began to disappear. He found out that since slavery wasn't considered very acceptable in the British Navy, he was treated much better and allowed to participate in the same sports and games as the white boys.

'Do you think the French will attack us soon?' Equiano asked. He was desperate for some excitement. The only French warship they'd spotted on their voyage had been in the English Channel, and had turned out to be a British ship in disguise! It was very disappointing.

'Maybe,' Richard replied. 'Then we'll capture their ships and be heroes! But first, I think our master is going to take us to London. He's going to receive a promotion.'

London. Equiano had heard a lot about the bustling city, and thought seeing it would be a great adventure. Yet by the time they arrived, he was too ill to see much at all!

'Perhaps we'll have to cut his leg off,' the surgeon of St. George's Hospital, London, said, frowning at Equiano's swollen feet. Due to the cold damp aboard the ship, his feet had become very red and very sore.

'No!' Equiano shouted, clutching at his left leg as if trying to pull it out of the doctor's sight.

'You have very bad chilblains, m'boy,' the surgeon said, shaking his head. 'See those blisters? That means there's been serious damage to your legs. In cases like this, amputation often becomes necessary.'

Happily, after several weeks in hospital, Equiano's chilblains began to heal. Unhappily, just as he was beginning to look forward to seeing London, he caught smallpox! Finally after eleven months, Equiano was released from hospital, but by then it was time to join his master on board a new ship.

War had been declared.

* * *

The sailor, looking up into the sky, swore terribly against God. At that moment, a piece of dirt fell into his eye. 'Ow!'

Equiano stepped back. *Was the great God in the heavens punishing the sailor?* That evening the sailor's eye was still red and swollen, and a week later, his eye had gone completely blind. Equiano shuddered when he heard the news. This great God is very powerful, he thought. I'd better be careful.

'Oi, Vassa!'

'Yes, sir?' Equiano entered his master's cabin.

Pascal folded his arms. Richard was standing by his side. 'You'd better say goodbye to Richard,' he said. 'He's going to stay aboard this ship, but I've been promoted again,' he pulled himself up proudly, 'this time to the *Royal George*.'

Richard! His best friend! Equiano flung himself into Richard's arms, and the two boys hugged. Richard had been kind and patient when no one else had bothered, and for four years now they had been firm friends.

As he waved goodbye to the friendly American boy, Equiano felt very alone. I don't have a single friend in the whole world now, he thought.

* * *

The *Royal George* turned out to be the biggest ship Equiano had ever seen. It was like a small floating village, and had taken ten years to build. But he was not aboard long before Pascal received another promotion.

On board the *Namur* Equiano travelled to Louisbourg, Nova Scotia. It was there that he finally witnessed a battle. How different it was to the fights he had watched from his tree in Africa! Instead of swords and spears there were huge exploding shells and many large guns. When the British eventually managed to repel the French soldiers, Equiano's ship was rigged with colour flags from the top of the mast all the way down to the deck in celebration.

Much later, Equiano found out that this battle had been a turning point in the Seven Years War, and marked the beginning of the end of French rule in Canada.

When winter came, Equiano found himself once more in England. Pascal, having business in London, sent Equiano to serve his cousins, the two Miss Guerins.

'So lovely to meet you, Gustavus,' the elder Miss Guerin said, when he arrived. 'My sister and I have been thinking – would you like to go to school, and learn to read and write?'

School? Equiano swelled with excitement. 'Yes, please!' he said. 'I want to learn everything.'

'Very well,' said Miss Guerin. 'We'll speak to a school master nearby, and see if you can join his class. And if you have any questions, you can always ask us. We would be happy to help you.'

And so began a very joyful period in Equiano's life. Each day the English world became less and less mysterious as he learnt more and more, both inside and outside the classroom. Now Richard was gone, Equiano was more grateful than ever to have people willing to answer his questions.

'What happens after we die?' He asked one of the servants in the Guerins' household, after he'd returned from school one afternoon.

'After you die?' The woman continued chopping carrots for dinner. 'Well... you go to live in a place called heaven. If you're baptised that is.'

'What's baptised?' Equiano asked.

'It's where you get splashed with water, and you become a Christian.'

Equiano frowned. While he'd certainly been splashed a lot with water while on board his master's ships, he was quite sure he wasn't a Christian. He rushed to the drawing room.

'Miss Guerin?'

'Yes, dear?'

Equiano folded and unfolded his hands as Miss Guerin put down her sewing.

'Can-I-be-baptised?'

Miss Guerin looked at him thoughtfully. Equiano continued to twist his hands. Finally she spoke. 'Yes, I spoke to your master Pascal about baptising you before, but he refused. I will speak to him again, he owes a debt to my brother, so he must let you be baptised if I insist.'

'Oh, thank you!' Equiano skipped out of the room, very relieved. *I am going to go to heaven!*

Before he was baptised the two Miss Guerins taught Equiano as much about God and Christianity as they could. They told him about the Ten Commandments and the importance of attending church. Finally, in

57

February 1759, Equiano was baptised in St Margaret's Church, Westminster. The minister gave him a book about Christianity, and the eldest Miss Guerin and her brother became his godparents. Afterwards they took him out for a treat. When they arrived home, Equiano was very happy. Now, he thought, I am a Christian. The great God who sends snow is no longer a stranger to me.

Before long, however, Equiano's master returned, and Equiano said a sad goodbye both to his schoolteacher and the two Guerin sisters. He was seaward bound once again!

Patrolling the oceans in an attempt to prevent the French from invading British soil, Equiano's ship stopped for a while at Gibraltar. There, Pascal called for him. 'Vassa!'

'Yes, master?'

'Richard's ship is going to dock here soon. We'll both see him again.'

Oh! Equiano waited with much excitement, until finally Richard's ship, which had come from Turkey, entered the harbour. How much he wanted to see his dear friend again! *I'll tell him that I can read a bit now, and I have been baptised just like the rest of the white men.*

Then the captain of Richard's ship came aboard, and behind him came some men carrying Richard's trunk, filled with his books and other items. Equiano frowned. Where was Richard?

'He's dead,' the captain said to Equiano's master. 'I brought you his belongings, since you were his officer.'

Equiano gasped and burst into tears. Richard, *dead?* Even when Pascal gave Richard's trunk to Equiano, he could not stop mourning. Richard had been more than a friend, he'd been a replacement for the family Equiano had lost. He wept for many days.

* * *

'The French are here!'

It was 7 o'clock in the evening when the cry went up. Equiano hurried out on deck, seeing the tall masts of the enemy fleet in the distance.

'Quick! Get the guns ready!' Equiano's ship and the others in the British fleet came alive with a swarm of activity. There were men everywhere, positioning the sails, lighting lanterns, tying cables, and preparing the weapons.

Equiano's ship surged out of the harbour, and chased the French until 4 pm the next day. As they approached the enemy fleet, Equiano's captain ordered everyone to lie on their stomachs on deck.

'The French will think we haven't noticed them because we won't seem ready for battle,' Equiano heard a sailor whisper, 'and then, when we're nice and close, we'll fire!'

And so it happened. As Equiano's ship came level to the French ship, all the men jumped up, ran to the guns, and fired them at the French. The French fired back and the whole sky quickly filled with smoke, the cannons thundering overhead, as Equiano ran up and down the slanting deck, carrying fresh gunpowder from the store room to the guns.

As a man was blown up beside him, Equiano froze in fear. Perhaps he should wait until the French were busy reloading their guns, before he made his next journey out into the open. Then he shook his head. No, he thought. God has given me a day to live and a day on which I will die. There's no point being afraid. What will come, will come. Besides, I'll have some incredible stories to tell Miss Guerin!

So he ran on, feet pounding on the slippery planks, continuing his work even when his master Pascal was injured and carried below deck. Then a rotten wooden box spilt grey gunpowder all over the deck, and Equiano and the other boys were kept busy, throwing water everywhere to prevent an unwanted explosion. By the time the naval battle drew to an end, Equiano was exhausted, and his ship was so torn up it had to be mended before they could sail back to England.

Still, they had survived!

* * *

'Oh!' Equiano stared down at the weathered Bible in his hands. 'But we do these things,' he said excitedly, 'we do these things!'

Daniel Queen, fellow-sailor, shook his head in amusement. 'What are you talking about, Vassa?'

Equiano jabbed his finger at the pages of the Bible his friend had been explaining to him. 'Circumcision. Washing at special times. Sacrifices with bitter herbs! All the things the Jews do, my people, the Igbo, do also!'

'Really?' Daniel Queen stared. A kind man in his forties, he had taken good care of Equiano from the moment Equiano and his master had boarded the *Aetna*, bound for Belle Ile. He had taught Equiano how to shave and do hair, as well as how to read the Bible. 'That's fascinating. Tell me more!'

Equiano told Daniel Queen all he remembered about his village and their customs, and the two men talked late into the night.

'Ah, my boy, you just wait,' said Daniel Queen as their lantern flickered in the darkness. 'Once this war's over, I'll teach you how to do business, and you'll be able to earn your own money and get all the education you want! We don't have slaves in the navy, and you can't have slaves on British soil. Your master will have to let you go.'

Equiano frowned. Pascal had told him many times that he had to be good and obedient in order for God to love him. If that was true, then Pascal would want to do good as well — and what could be more good than setting Equiano free after all the years he had served him? Equiano smiled, hope burning in his throat. 'Do you think —'

'Oh! Oh!' The cry came from overhead. Queen and Equiano jumped to their feet.

'Oh!' A voice came echoing down to them. 'I had a terrible dream! The apostle Peter appeared and told me I ought to repent, because time is very short. Oh! He showed me awful things!'

'Is that John Mondle?' asked Equiano. Mondle was known for his bad character, and it was very surprising that he should be worried about eternity. Besides, it was 4 o'clock in the morning!

'Sounds like it,' said Queen.

'Cheer up, man.' They heard the sailor keeping watch laugh. 'It was just a dream!'

'No!' came Mondle's voice, 'No! I must change my life!'

There was the sound of someone running, and then Mondle burst into the mess room where Queen and Equiano were talking.

'Here!' he said, thrusting bottles of alcohol towards them. 'Take it! I must change my life. I am going to read my Bible right now!'

He was gone before they could reply. 'Come on,' Queen said, picking up their lantern. 'We should get some rest.'

* * *

A few hours later, at seven thirty that morning, Equiano was awake, thinking over what Queen had said last night. Freedom. A business of his own. An education —

'Oh! Lord have mercy!'

'Save us!'

The cries came from the sailors on deck. Equiano jumped to his feet and ran out into the ship corridor. Mondle, still awake, also heard the distant cries, and came running out of his cabin. Four seconds later, there was a gigantic crashing sound, and the hull of a nearby ship smashed into the side of Equiano's ship – crushing Mondle's cabin to smithereens.

Equiano stared at Mondle, who was wiping blood off his face, where a small piece of wood had struck him. Mr Mondle stared back. 'I – I almost died,' the frightened man said. 'I – if I hadn't been awake because of my dream, I wouldn't have heard the cries.'

Wow, thought Equiano, amazed. God really does interfere in everyday life to save people. But what does this mean for me?

A while later, walking across the upper deck of the Aetna, Equiano slipped and fell down to the bottom hold — many, many metres below. He landed with a loud thump on the wooden deck.

'Oh!' a sailor cried.

'He's dead,' another said.

Equiano, cheek rubbing against the rough wood, lifted his head, pulled himself to his knees, and tried to catch his breath.

He should have been killed from such a fall — but instead, as he soon discovered, not even a single bone was broken! Getting shakily to his feet, Equiano remembered what Daniel Queen had taught him. *Not even the smallest sparrow falls without God's permission.*

It really was true!

* * *

The battle between French and British forces on the island of Belle Ile was fierce and long. Many times Equiano only barely managed to escape with his life from exploding mortars or French soldiers. Once a wild horse almost threw him over a cliff! Throughout it all Equiano clung onto two hopes — the God of heaven was real and had planned out his life, and very soon he would be a free man.

When the battle finally ended with the British taking control of the island, everyone celebrated with great cries of joy! Equiano jiggled in excitement as his ship neared England. The war was ending and freedom was so close!

Back to the West Indies

'No,' said Equiano's master, Pascal, grabbing hold of his elbow, and dragging Equiano toward a rowboat. 'You're not going onto English soil. You will try and escape – and I won't let you!'

Equiano blinked, confused. Why would he try to sneak away? What rumours had Pascal heard?

'Shall I fetch my books and clothes?' he asked at last. Wherever Pascal wanted to take him, he didn't want to leave his hard-won belongings behind.

Pascal gave a harsh laugh. 'I'm not falling for that trick! If you go out of my sight for even one second, I will cut your throat.' He drew his sword.

Equiano tried to pull away. 'But you can't! I'm free on English soil!'

Pascal swore. 'You're not free until I say you're free!' he shouted.

The truth was, the law about slavery in England was very confusing. There was no law which automatically made slaves on English soil free. Some law courts let slaves go free, and others did not. Many people, like

Daniel Queen, believed that slavery could not exist in Britain, yet the newspapers held advertisements for slave sales, and notices for the return of runaway slaves. The British Navy, however, frowned upon slavery, and so Equiano had been treated like the other boys aboard during the Seven Years War.

Pascal pushed Equiano into the rowboat, and the tide immediately began to pull them down the Thames. 'Row!' Equiano's master yelled at the other sailors. 'I will find a slave ship bound for the West Indies,' he told Equiano, 'and I will sell you.'

'Please!' begged Equiano.

'We are tired!' protested the sailors, secretly on Equiano's side. 'We can't row much further!'

'No,' said the first few captains they rowed past, as Pascal shouted from his rowboat up to their ships. 'No, we don't want him.'

Equiano began to feel hopeful. Perhaps Pascal's plan would fail. Perhaps —

'Yes,' said Captain Doran, of the *Charming Sally*. 'Come aboard, I'll buy him.'

Pascal shouted at his sailors to stop rowing and dragged Equiano onboard and into the captain's cabin.

Captain Doran looked down his nose at Equiano. 'You are my slave now.'

'No,' said Equiano, terrified by the thought of being whisked away from England, from Daniel Queen, and from the kind Guerin sisters. 'My master cannot sell me.'

'Why not? Didn't he buy you?'

'Yes,' Equiano confessed, 'but I have worked hard for him for eight years and he has taken all my wages and all my prize money from the war, and I have been baptised, and Christians do not sell other Christians, and I heard a lawyer say that slavery is not allowed in Britain!'

Captain Doran snorted at Equiano's desperate list of reasons. 'You talk too much,' he said, 'and if you do not behave yourself and stay quiet, I have many ways to make you obey me.'

Equiano, in a flash, remembered his last voyage on a slave ship – the bruising chains, the dizzying hunger, the suffocating stench – and shuddered. With a sinking heart he realised that all the skills and experience he had acquired since then meant nothing. He was an African, and that meant he was powerless.

Equiano gathered his courage and looked his new master in the eye. 'Even though I may never receive any justice here on earth, I will certainly get it in heaven,' he said, and walked out of the cabin.

Equiano watched Pascal's rowboat until it disappeared up the Thames. Pascal had even taken his coat from him, so he stood and shivered in his shirt, and when his old master was gone, he slumped to the deck and wept.

Will I ever be free? Equiano remembered swearing that when he returned to England he would spend the whole day gambling with the rest of the sailors. Is this new slavery a punishment from God? Please, Lord, he prayed, do not abandon me!

After a while Equiano began to remember what he'd learnt from the Bible. He recalled all the times his life had been spared in dangerous situations. God is looking after me, he decided. He thought of the prophecy made at his birth, and the promise God makes to all Christians, to work all things for their good. Finally, he got up from the deck, and wiped away his tears. *God can deliver me, even now.*

Yet on 30 December, when the ship sailed out of the English harbour and Equiano was still a prisoner on board, his hope began to sink. *I wish they had never named me the fortunate one! Why must my destiny be so terrible? Why are God's plans for me so painful?*

* * *

'Land!'

Montserrat, an island in the West Indies known for its sugar, cacao and rum production, came into view, and Equiano swallowed. This was his new life — one of labouring beneath the hot sun, being whipped by overseers, and sold from master to master until he died.

'Oi! Unload the ship!'

For days Equiano toiled unloading and reloading the merchant ship. Unused to the hot sun, often dashed against the side of the boat by the rough waves, he was soon bruised, torn, and sunburnt. Still, he worked hard. *Perhaps Captain Doran will take me back to England with him!*

'Vassa! Come here!' Captain Doran was with a man Equiano had not seen before. 'I've just sold you to Mr. King for forty pounds,' he told twenty-one-year-old Equiano. 'He's a good man, and I've told him you're a good worker.'

'Oh, please! Oh, sir! Won't you take me back to England?'

'Come now,' said Mr King, from beside the captain. 'I will treat you well. I'm from Philadelphia, and I can send you to school there. You can work as a clerk.'

It was a small promise, and one which would never be filled, but Equiano needed all the hope he could get when Captain Doran's boat left for England, leaving him behind in a strange land. Besides, although Equiano often went hungry, Mr King was indeed a kind master compared to the other white men on Montserrat.

* * *

'Pull!'

Equiano heaved on the oar with the other slaves, trying to direct the boat safely into the small harbour. As a merchant, Mr King sent small boats in between the islands of the West Indies, trading and collecting rum, sugar and other goods to sell in America.

Pulling on the oars, sometimes for sixteen hours a day, was exhausting work – but Equiano knew he was lucky. Not only did Mr King give him some food each day, but he also provided food for the other slaves, whose masters, to try and earn as much money as possible, hired them out as rowers but didn't give them enough food. At that moment the hired slave beside him sighed.

'Are you alright?' Equiano asked, as they rowed.

'No. There's no such thing as right, on these terrible islands,' said the man. He was silent for a while. 'I went fishing last night, even though we only got a few hours rest.'

'Did you catch anything?'

'I caught a few,' the man sighed. 'But my master took them before I could sell them.'

'Did he pay you?'

The man laughed. 'Of course not. And if he doesn't take them, another white man'll come along and take them. Then I go to my master, and he comes and takes them off the white man, but keeps them himself. What am I supposed to do? If my master is unjust, there is no one else to go to.' The man looked up at the blazing sun. 'There is no justice here. I can only look to the God up top for that.'

Equiano's stomach gurgled at the thought of fish. 'Keep looking to God up there,' he encouraged. 'He's our only chance of justice.'

The man stared at the dull, smudgy horizon. 'I've been sold from man to man since I was born, Vassa. I've been taken from my wife, from my children.' He bent over the oar. 'I'm so tired.'

* * *

Soon Mr King began to allow Equiano to go on longer voyages on his ships. He did not want to at first, afraid Equiano would run away, but the ship's captain promised he would keep a close eye on the young man.

As he travelled from island to island and even worked on slave ships completing the same voyage to America he had once been on, Equiano saw greater horrors than any he'd seen before.

Slaves were locked in tiny boxes for hours on end as a punishment; they were burnt with candles; they had their ears cut to shreds bit by bit; they slept in open sheds in damp places, and no one helped them when they were ill. Pregnant women were treated just as badly, and most of them lost their babies. When new female slaves were brought aboard the ship, Equiano had to turn away, because he knew he could not stop the sailors from mistreating them.

Everywhere he looked, he saw men claiming to be Christians hurting their fellow men, selling them for sixpence per pound, and every day he was more and more grateful to God for Mr King.

'A glass, please.' Equiano said.

'Just one? You can get two for cheaper.'

'Just one, please,' Equiano told the trader on the island of St Eustatius. He had managed to get hold of three pence, and could only afford one drinking glass. *Please Lord, let this be the beginning of my freedom.*

Back in Montserrat, Equiano sold the glass for sixpence, and the next time his boat went to St Eustatia, he bought two drinking glasses. He continued his trading as he went about his master's business and in six weeks he'd managed to make sixty pence. *All praise to you, God, for my riches!*

* * *

Equiano boarded the boat, two lumpy bags pressed tightly to his chest. Beside him, his fisherman friend clutched a similar bag.

'I really think this time we have a chance,' said the other slave. 'I've heard oranges and limes sell well on St Croix, and they're so easy to buy here in Montserrat.'

'I hope so,' said Equiano. He'd spent all the money he'd managed to make so far on these fruits.

When they landed on the island and the work for the day was over, the two men went ashore to sell their fruit.

'Give them here!' Without warning, two white men met them on the sand, and snatched the heavy bags from their arms.

'No! Please!' Equiano tried to understand. Perhaps the men were only joking, and would give the fruits back.

The white men laughed, and walked off with the bags. Equiano and his friend followed them all the way to the fort. 'Please! Please give them back! The fruit is ours!'

'Go away!' shouted one of the white men, turning around with a furious expression on his face. 'We want them, and if you keep begging, we'll whip you!'

'But those bags you are holding, they're all we have in the world,' begged Equiano. 'Even our clothes are given by our masters, but we bought these with our own money. We came to sell them.'

The white men picked up sticks. Equiano and his friend had no choice but to leave in a daze. All their months of hard work – gone. What could they do?

'Please,' they said to the commanding officers at the fort. 'Our fruit has been stolen by two men —'

'You good-for-nothing trouble makers!' spat an officer, picking up a horse-whip. 'Why would we believe you?'

Equiano and his friend ran. 'There must be something else we can do!' said the fisherman.

Back at the house of the two white men, Equiano and his fellow slave continued their cries. 'Please! Return our fruit!'

Finally, tired by their shouts, some of the other members of the household came out. 'We will give you two bags back,' they said. 'Now go away.'

The two bags were Equiano's. Afraid they would change their mind, he took them and ran back to the ship as fast as he could. His friend was not so lucky, and lost everything he owned. 'Oh God!' he cried, stretching his hands to the sky. 'When will justice come? When will you help me?'

Equiano gave him some of his fruit, and they went to sell what they had at the market. They got a surprisingly good price for their goods, and Equiano felt like he was in a dream. One moment all had been lost, and now he was holding just over two pounds in coin! *I can trust you in any situation, can't I, Lord?*

Finally, on a journey to St Kitt's Equiano was able, with a loan from the captain, to buy a Bible. He opened it that night with a wide smile. He'd lost his own when Pascal had sold him, and had not seen a single one for sale on Montserrat. But now he had God's Word in his hands once again.

* * *

'Vassa! Come here!'

Equiano entered Mr King's house in Montserrat. 'Yes, master?'

'I heard you were planning on running away on the coming voyage to Philadelphia,' Mr King said with a frown. 'Well, I won't have that, so I'm going to sell you to Captain Doran's brother-in-law.'

Equiano gaped. Captain Doran's brother-in-law was well known for his cruelty, and had tried several times to buy him, but Mr King had always refused, and Equiano had worked extra hard to make sure Mr King would keep him. 'But master,' he said, 'I was not planning on running away! You have been kind to me, and I wanted to obtain my freedom legally. Please —' he turned to Captain Farmer, who had sailed with Equiano all this time, 'have I ever tried to escape?'

'He has never tried to escape,' Captain Farmer told Mr King. 'Sometimes I pretended I wasn't watching him, to see if he would try, but he never did. Even when some of the white sailors abandoned us, and invited him to join them, he stayed with the ship.' The captain shook his head. 'I think the rumour you heard has come from the mate, who dislikes your slave, because your slave caught him stealing provisions from the ship.'

'Yes, you are right, he is a good fellow.' Mr King looked at Equiano. 'That's the reason I've let him carry on his little trades. Well!' Mr King dug in his pocket for a silver coin. 'Perhaps I've been too quick to listen to lies. You may have this, Vassa, to help with your trades, and once you've earnt forty pounds, you can buy your freedom.'

Forty Pounds for a Life

Equiano soaked in his first view of Philadelphia, the 'city of brotherly love', with a heart full of gratitude. Whenever he thought of his master's promise, his chest expanded with so much joy that it hurt. *Soon, so soon, I will be free.*

To add to his delight, he was able to get good prices for his wares in this American city and no one tried to take them from him unfairly.

'Hey, Vassa,' said a sailor one evening. 'Have you heard of Mrs Davies? She's a wise woman, she can tell you your future.'

Equiano shook his head. Fortune-telling was against the Bible. After all, who but God could know the path of his life?

That night, however, he had a vivid dream of a woman. Could it be the wise woman? All day as he worked he could not stop thinking of his dream. He remembered the dream of Mr Mondle, and how it had seemed to be from God.

'Alright,' he said that night to the sailor. 'Where does Mrs Davies live?'

On following the sailor's directions, Equiano met Mrs Davies – and she was the woman he had seen in his dream, wearing the exact same dress, even though he had never seen her before!

'Let me tell you about your life so far,' Mrs Davies said, and as she spoke, Equiano grew even more astonished because everything she said was correct. Eventually she said, 'You will not be a slave for long. Within the next eighteen months you will be twice in great danger, but if you survive you will see great success.'

Equiano liked the idea of not being a slave for much longer! He left her, mind buzzing. Could this be from God?

After Philadelphia, Equiano and his ship went back to the West Indies, loaded up on slaves, and then sailed back to America, this time to Georgia.

'Oh, you look ill!'

Equiano tossed and turned on his bunk on the ship, sweat dripping down his face. Very keen to prove he was too valuable to sell, and wanting to get his freedom soon, he had been doing the work of two men for months. He had worn himself out, and caught a bad fever.

He remembered the wise woman's words. Was he to die here, before gaining his freedom? Fear struck him. As a child he had thought baptism would get him to heaven, but now he was filled with doubts. After all, the cruel slave owners were baptised. Would they go to heaven? Oh Lord, Equiano begged from his sickbed. If you heal me, I promise I will be good!

Captain Farmer fetched a well-known doctor, and after lying ill for eleven days, Equiano finally recovered. When he arrived back at Montserrat, however, he forgot his promise, and began to swear again and live in selfish ways.

His work for Mr King next took him to Charleston, where Equiano found that the merchants were not fair like the ones in Philadelphia. Instead they took his wares and refused to pay him, or paid him in bad money, for which he just managed to avoid a whipping in the marketplace.

Afterwards the ship stopped in Georgia. There he made some friends among the slaves, and visited them in their master's yard.

'Ah, look, Master's just come home.'

'He's drunk! Maybe you should —'

'What's this! A strange black man?' Before Equiano could explain that he was just visiting, and that his captain knew Dr Perkins, he was struck across the face.

'Please, sir,' Equiano raised his hands. 'Forgive me, have mercy. I didn't —'

'I'll give you what you deserve, you lying ruffian!' Dr Perkins and his white servant began to beat Equiano, until he fell to the ground, almost dead. In fact, he lost so much blood he was unable to move. They left him there all night, and in the morning dragged him to jail.

'Vassa!' Captain Farmer came rushing in. 'Where have you been – oh!' At the sight of Equiano's torn body, the shocked captain held his hand to his mouth.

'Oh, what have they done?' he moaned, tears slipping down into his beard. He immediately took Equiano back to his lodging house, and sent for the best doctors he could find.

'He's too far gone,' said one.

'He won't recover,' said the other. 'Best buy another slave.'

It was sixteen days before Equiano was able to get out of bed, but thanks to Captain Farmer, who nursed him all through the night, he was at least able to do that.

'It's infuriating!' the captain complained, storming up and down in front of Equiano's bed. 'The court said they would do nothing, because you're black. Dr Perkins refused to duel me, because he's a coward, even though that's how we often settle problems. How am I supposed to get my revenge? We need you working on board, not lying here half-dead because some man with a reputation for cruelty decided he didn't like your face!'

Despite the captain's frustrations, it was four weeks before Equiano was well enough to reboard the ship and sail back to Montserrat. By then he too was frustrated – he wanted to go on more voyages and earn his freedom as quickly as possible!

* * *

'Sir?' Equiano said to Captain Farmer, after many more voyages from the West Indies to the American colonies. 'I have earned forty-seven pounds.'

'Congratulations, boy!'

'How should I buy my freedom?' Equiano asked, remembering how Captain Farmer had defended his character to Mr King a year earlier.

'Hmm,' the Captain rubbed his beard. 'On 11 July I am having breakfast with your master. Go to him then.'

Equiano, terrified with the weight of his expectations, woke up on the morning of the 11th with a fluttering stomach. He got ready as best he could and then made his way to his master's dining room. There he bowed deeply and entered, unable to stop trembling. He held out his money. 'Please, master. Here is the money, please honour your promise to me.'

'What?' Mr King sat back in his chair, stunned. Equiano's heart sank. 'Give you your freedom?' Mr. King demanded. 'Where on earth did you get that money? Do you have forty whole pounds?'

'Yes, sir.' Equiano said. Would his master change his mind after all this?

'Where did you get it from?' Mr King asked sharply.

'Very honestly,' replied Equiano.

'It's true,' Captain Farmer interrupted. 'I've seen him work very hard and make very careful investments.'

'Well!' Mr King grumbled. 'He makes money faster than me! I certainly would not have promised him his freedom if I thought he would get the money so soon.'

'Come, come!' Captain Farmer clapped Mr King on the back, 'You really must let him have his freedom. He has earnt you more than a hundred pounds a year, and he will earn you more. He will not leave you just because he is free. Come now, take the money.'

Mr King sighed. 'I'd better keep my promise, I suppose.' He took the money from Equiano's outstretched hands. 'Go on, go to the Register Office and ask them to write up a manumission paper for you. I'll sign it.'

To Equiano, Mr King's agreement was like a voice from heaven. All his fears were swept away in a flood of absolute happiness. He bowed deeply, eyes overflowing, unable to speak.

'Congratulations!' shouted Captain Farmer, to the room at large. 'Congratulations!'

'Thank you – thank you – thank you!' babbled Equiano, and then ran to the Register Office. God had saved him! *Thank you, Lord!* It all felt like a dream, and by the time Equiano arrived at the office, he was dizzy and out of breath because he'd stopped to tell everyone he'd met on the way about his great good fortune!

'The papers cost a pound,' the man at the desk said. Then he looked at Equiano's huge smile. 'But I'll do it for half price – congratulations!'

That morning Equiano had been a slave, and, according to his manumission papers, his 'lord and master' Mr King had held all 'right, title, dominion, sovereignty and property,' over him. Now, by evening, he was a 'Freedman', with a certificate to prove it.

The elderly black people of Montserrat blessed him with prayers and joyful words, and the younger Africans joined Equiano as he danced in jubilation. The Lord has done great things for me, he thought, remembering Psalm 126. I am, once more, a fortunate one!

* * *

'We'd like you to still work on our ship,' said Captain Farmer and Mr King. 'Do not leave us.'

What could Equiano do? He wanted very much to go to London and leave the West Indies forever, but he felt immensely grateful for the freedom they had given him.

'Very well,' he said. I will make a voyage or two, he thought, and then go to England.

Equiano soon discovered that being a free man did not make much difference in the way white people treated him. His word was still not accepted in court. The laws of the American colonies he visited seemed to only protect those with white skin. Once in Georgia he was forced to hide for five days in the house of a friend, because a cruel merchant had convinced the police he ought to be whipped. Even Captain Farmer did not feel the need to treat him fairly – after all, who could Equiano go to for justice? Not the police.

'You can take two bulls aboard to sell this voyage,' Captain Farmer said. Equiano, cheered by the money to be made by selling the large animals, worked harder than ever to load the ship.

'May I fetch my two bulls now, Captain?' he asked when everything was ready.

Captain Farmer shook his head. 'There's no room.'

Equiano was dismayed. 'Can I bring one bull, then?'

'No,' said the captain.

'But you gave me your word!' Equiano protested. He remembered the rights which were his now, little as they were. 'I will leave the ship.'

The captain, thinking of the sick mate whose work Equiano was doing for no extra pay, began to get nervous. 'We need you, Vassa! Do not be offended. You can take as many turkeys and other birds as you like.'

'But I've never traded turkeys before,' Equiano said. 'They will never last the voyage back to the West Indies.'

'Just give it a try,' the captain urged. 'Come on. If they die I will give you money.'

It seems I will make less money on my first voyage as a free man than all my trips as a slave! Equiano thought. Still, he had little choice, and brought four dozen birds on board.

When the captain brought his own bulls onto the ship, one escaped and butted him viciously in the chest. Already injured, once the ship sailed he fell ill with the same sickness as the mate.

'Pump the water out!' The sea was very rough, and the ship began taking on water. Equiano, who had never been taught navigation for fear he would use it to escape, became the makeshift captain. As they journeyed they were forced to pump water out of the bottom of the ship every half an hour. Meanwhile the captain grew sicker and sicker, until at last he called Equiano to his side.

'I am dying,' he said, and perhaps feeling guilty, asked, 'Have I ever done you any harm?'

'Oh,' said Equiano, remembering how the captain had tended him night and day when he'd been badly beaten, and convinced Mr King to let him go free. 'Oh, I would be an ungrateful wretch if I thought so!'

When the captain died, everyone wept because he had been greatly loved. Equiano grieved deeply – realising that if the captain had died just five months earlier, he never would have obtained his freedom.

As Equiano steered their boat into the port at Montserrat, he found that while every single one of the captain's bulls had died in the storm, all of his turkeys, despite being on deck during the terrible weather, had survived.

This is your hand at work, God! Equiano rejoiced. I would have lost everything if the captain had kept his promise.

'Vassa navigated all the way back to Montserrat!' exclaimed everyone who heard the story. 'Incredible! We'll have to call him Captain Vassa from now on!'

* * *

Now the captain was dead, Equiano turned his thoughts to London. But Mr King had other ideas.

'I've got a new captain,' he said, 'but the mate is still ill and there's no one else – please go on another journey to Georgia.'

Vassa sighed, but felt unable to refuse.

On board, though, he soon realised that this new captain meant to travel a different way to America. 'I have proper skill,' the new captain boasted. 'This is the best way!'

A few days after they began their journey, Equiano had a strange dream. He dreamt the ship was shipwrecked on the rocks, and he was the only one who could save everyone on board.

'How strange!' Equiano laughed the next morning as he began work.

That night, however, he dreamt the same dream.

'How strange!' he laughed again, and continued his work. Yet later that day, tired and frustrated, Equiano swore at a piece of machinery. Immediately, he felt bad. Sorry, Lord, he prayed, I shouldn't have lost my temper.

That night, as soon as he fell asleep he dreamed the exact same dream as before. At midnight, when he got up for his watch shift, one of the sailors called him over. 'Look! A whale.'

Equiano frowned at the moonlight dancing on the waves. 'That's not a whale. That's a rock!' He rushed to wake the captain.

'I'm coming! I'm coming!' grumbled the captain – but he did not come.

Equiano hurried down below deck again. 'Captain! The current is carrying us straight towards the rock! Please come!'

'I'm coming!' shouted the captain. But he did not come.

On deck, Equiano saw that they were even closer to the rock. Furious now, he ran back down below deck. 'Captain!' he yelled. 'Why aren't you coming? The ship is almost on the rock!'

Finally, the captain came on deck, but by now it was too late. The current was too strong, the ship could not be turned, and the moment they lifted the anchor, the ship struck the rock with a loud crash.

Horror made Equiano freeze on the slanting deck beneath the moon and the growling waves. Was this God's punishment for his curse? He had, after all, sworn against the ship, on which his life depended! He saw all his sins laid out in front of him. *Oh Lord, if we are saved, I will never swear again!* As the waves growled all around him, Equiano remembered the multitude of ways God had delivered him in the past. *Perhaps God will rescue me once more.*

'Lock the slaves below deck!' shouted the captain.

Equiano stared. All the slaves would surely die if the hatches were nailed down — and if this shipwreck was his fault, their blood would be on his head!

'No! Stop!'

'I won't have them taking up space in our small escape boat!' the captain roared.

Equiano spluttered. 'We wouldn't have to worry about it if you'd navigated properly!' he shouted back. Because the rest of the sailors were also unhappy at the captain, Equiano was not punished for his anger, and the slaves were not locked below deck. From then on, Equiano took charge and managed to bring everyone safely ashore to a deserted island in the Bahamas, where he planted some oranges and limes as a gift to any shipwrecked sailors in the future.

Once more God was kind, and Equiano, the captain, the sailors and the slaves were rescued by a passing boat just as their water supply ran out. Now, thought Equiano, as they left the Bahamas behind, I have certainly repaid Mr King, and I will leave the West Indies at once!

Knocking at the Door

But getting back to England was not so simple. Equiano had lent some money to a white captain who refused to return it, and so he was forced to sail with the man until he decided to give it back. Then he was not allowed to leave St Kitts before he had advertised his leaving — just in case he was a slave trying to escape!

Most ships sailing to England departed the islands by late July, and as each day passed, Equiano grew more and more impatient. He didn't want to miss his chance!

At long last, with great pleasure, he watched the West Indies grow small on the horizon.

'Miss Guerin!' On arriving safely in England, Equiano immediately went to visit his old friends. It was a wonderful reunion, and Equiano told them all about his adventures. Then he bumped into Captain Pascal.

'How did you get back here?' demanded the captain, astonished.

'In a ship,' said Equiano, remembering how the captain had so cruelly sold him without even the coat on his back.

'Obviously,' spat Pascal, 'I didn't think you walked to London on the water.'

'Captain,' Equiano said, 'I was very faithful to you, and you were very unkind to me.'

Pascal turned and walked away.

A few days later, Equiano again met the captain, this time at the Guerins' house. 'Captain? Could I now at least have the prize money which was mine from serving in the war?' He had a new life to begin in London, after all.

Pascal snorted. 'Even if your prize money had been ten thousand pounds, I have a right to all of it. If you're really bothered, you can take me to court!' He laughed, thinking that Equiano would never be able to afford a lawyer.

'I will!' said Equiano, and Pascal grew even more furious. Still, thought Equiano, it would not be kind to the two Guerin sisters if he took their cousin to court – so he did nothing.

Equiano kept busy in his first few years as a free man. By this time in his late twenties, he paid tutors to instruct him in mathematics, hairdressing and how to play the French horn. He went on many more voyages and was finally taught navigation. He lived in Turkey for five months, and enjoyed it very much. The Muslims there treated him kindly and even invited him to stay and live among them.

In 1773 Equiano joined an expedition to the Arctic. He came on board the *Racehorse* as the servant of Mr Charles Irving, a Scottish inventor who had developed a method to make salt water fresh. The Royal Navy's Arctic expedition was led by the man who would become Lord Mulgrave, and the goal was to discover a passage through the North Pole to India.

'Look!' Equiano laughed in amazement at the sky, which was as bright as morning even though it was the middle of the night.

The sailor beside him grinned. 'Impossible, isn't it? I thought the fellows who told me the sun never sets in Greenland were joking!'

On either side of their creaking ship rose high mountains of ice, glowing blue and translucent in the sun. Huge, dark whales breathed clouds of water into the air, and noisy walruses, their ivory tusks glinting against the deep cerulean sea, clambered around the ship, evading capture.

'No, it's not good,' a Greenland captain said, coming aboard the *Racehorse* from his own vessel, one day. 'There are three ships lost on the ice – it's very dangerous out there.'

Still, the expedition pressed on, holding their northward course.

'Ice!' The cry went up on 11th July. Equiano leaned over the ship's rail – all he could see ahead of them was one long stretch of frozen water. What would they do now?

The ship changed direction slightly, and sailed beside the ice for just over two weeks. Still the white sheet stretched out before them all the way to the horizon, with no way through.

'We'll tie up here for a while.' The constant sunshine and the dazzling beauty of the ice made the men feel like they were on holiday! The sun, reflected off the white landscape, turned the clouds all sorts of brilliant hues, and there was plenty to see.

'Look! Bears!' As the huge polar bears lumbered into view, the sailors managed to hunt down nine of them. While some of the men relished the fresh meat, Equiano thought they were rather stringy! The walruses were not so happy being hunted, and attacked one of the rowboats, stealing an oar from a sailor.

On 1st August, Equiano heard a loud creaking sound.

'Both our ships are stuck in the ice!' The news spread, and for seven days the men on the expedition cast worried glances at the ice sheets, hoping they would soon break free. Finally they held a council.

'The ice is going to squeeze our ships to pieces.'

'Perhaps we can walk across the ice, dragging our ships to water?'

But the distance proved to be too far. The men went around with heavy hearts. 'This is it. There's no hope!'

They sawed at the ice around the ship, in an attempt to keep the ships from being crushed. Equiano was hard at work when he slipped on the ice and tumbled into the icy water.

'Help! Help! I can't swim!' The water was paralysingly cold, and Equiano, weighed down by his thick clothes, began to sink.

'Here! Catch hold of this!' As he was dragged out of the water, Equiano's thoughts turned once again to eternity. If these men hadn't happened to be walking by, he would have perished. *Am I ready to die?*

With death haunting the explorers at every turn, Equiano became increasingly convinced that he was not.

Perhaps the same fears plagued the other men on the expedition, because soon even men who had previously used God's name in vain began to pray in desperation for deliverance. They prayed and prayed, until one day the wind suddenly changed direction and the ice began to shatter. Thirty hours later the ships on the expedition were back in open water and heading back to London.

The Lord has saved us! Equiano marvelled. He heard our prayers!

* * *

Back in England, Equiano was greatly troubled. I have to try harder, he thought, tossing and turning at night. If I had died on the ice I would not have gone to heaven. I've been too sinful. I have to be a better Christian!

Worried, he began attending church up to three times a day. Yet after many weeks, he still had no relief.

I'll go to the Quakers, he thought. Quakers were Christians who held different beliefs to the Church of England, yet Mr King and many of the merchants in Philadelphia had been Quakers, and were far kinder to

Equiano than other men. Remembering this, Equiano went to one of their meetings. He left even more confused, because no one had read the Bible aloud.

Next he went to the Roman Catholics, but their teachings could not bring him peace either. With the fear of eternity plaguing his mind daily, Equiano went to visit the Jews. 'How can I escape the coming wrath?' he asked, but still was not given a satisfactory answer.

Back in his lodging house, Equiano decided to read the four Gospels, Mathew, Mark, Luke and John, from start to finish, and then join whichever religion agreed with them. Yet every person he asked seemed to give different answers to his many questions, and he could not find a single one who kept all the Ten Commandments! I have only ever managed to keep eight out of ten commandments, Equiano thought, because I work on Sundays and swear sometimes, yet I do better than my friends — and still, I do not feel sure I am saved.

One day, tired of his daily troubles and fears, Equiano made a decision. *I will go to Turkey to seek salvation. The Muslims there were more honest than many of the Christians I have met, so perhaps their way to heaven is the right one.*

'Yes, we need a steward,' agreed Captain John Hughes. 'And do you know of a cook we can employ?'

'John Annis,' replied Equiano, 'is a free black man and a very clever cook.'

Yet before they could leave for Turkey, Annis was kidnapped from the ship by a former master on Easter Monday.

'You must help him!' Equiano implored Captain Hughes, 'or at least give me some of the wages he has already earnt, so I can procure his release.'

The captain refused.

In an attempt to bring John Annis' former master to court, Equiano went to Granville Sharp, the famous abolitionist for advice. Two years earlier, Granville Sharp had succeeded in forcing the law court to acknowledge at last that slavery could not be upheld in England, and slaves could not be removed from British soil without their consent. The ruling came ten years too late for Equiano's 1762 kidnapping, but he hoped it would work in John Annis' favour.

But it was not to be. Equiano's lawyer proved unfaithful, taking his money without doing any work, and John Annis was shipped to the West Indies against his will, where he was horribly mistreated, and died before help could arrive.

All seemed dark now for Equiano. What sort of place was the world, if even the law could not prevent John Annis from falling into evil hands? Equiano felt utterly helpless in the face of the slave trade and racism which prevailed in the Western countries and their colonies. His sins, too, seemed to pile up in every direction he turned, and eternity appeared full of fearful punishment.

Why have you given me so much misfortune, God? Equiano cried out. Deciding he would leave England entirely, he tried to board another ship for Turkey, but Captain Hughes would not let him.

Thwarted at every turn, Equiano began to grumble and blaspheme. But that too brought no relief, and he fell down on his knees. *Give me more time Lord! Just give me more time to repent and be good!*

God granted him more time, and Equiano continued to pray. You have given me many talents, Lord. Why have I not used them better? I should have done all to glorify you! Why won't you make me holier so I can get to heaven?

Wanting only to spend the entire day reading his Bible, Equiano felt he could not do so at his lodging place, where he could hear people using God's name in vain. He walked the streets restlessly, until he bumped into an old sailor. They began speaking, and the man told him how the love of God had changed his heart. Equiano spoke for a long time with the old sailor in his house, until a Methodist minister arrived.

'Have you ever heard the gospel preached?' the minister asked, in response to Equiano's eager questions.

Equiano frowned. 'I don't know what you mean by 'the gospel',' he said. 'I've read the gospel accounts in the Bible?'

'Come with me to my chapel,' the minister said. 'We are having a love feast this evening.'

Understanding that the old sailor and the minister had a sort of faith that he wanted desperately, Equiano went along to the chapel that evening. He had been expecting a party, with a feast of food and drink — but instead there were hymns and prayers and finally communion. It was this meeting the Methodists called a 'love feast'. It was very different to the churches Equiano had visited previously, which had relied on strict forms and rituals.

'God has been very good to me,' one of the congregation said.

Equiano nodded, God had saved him many times too.

'I am so thankful I can be certain of heaven, and that nothing can tear me from the hands of God.'

Equiano stared, surprised and a bit jealous! If only he could say words like that, and know they were true. These Christians must be far more holy than him!

The meeting lasted four hours, and afterwards Equiano was sure of one thing: He wanted to be as happy as these people. He went back to his lodging house troubled, but determined to entirely give up the card-playing and coarse jokes of sailors. Time, he felt, was very short, and eternity very long and very near.

The next day he returned to the old sailor and his wife, who lent him a Christian book with questions and answers about faith. 'Come and visit us whenever you want!' they called, as he left after many hours of discussion.

Two months passed, and Equiano slowly began to learn the gospel truths for the first time.

'It does not matter how many commandments you keep,' a minister told him. 'You must have your sins taken away by the blood of Jesus.'

Equiano staggered. *That's too easy.* 'But how can I know my sins are forgiven?' he demanded.

'God must tell you.'

'This is all very mysterious,' Equiano muttered. 'I want something straightforward!'

'It is straightforward,' the minister said. 'The Bible says that if you call on God your sins will be forgiven. Ask God, and he will show you the state of your soul.'

But how can I be sure? Equiano pondered. At least if I try to keep the commandments I can see that I am working. Next he went to Westminster Chapel, and there the minister said he was going to ask people questions before they joined communion.

I'm not sure if I'm good enough to join, Equiano thought, but I'll try anyway. 'I keep eight out of ten commandments,' he told the minister.

'Have you read the Bible?' asked the minister. 'Even one sin means you cannot get into heaven, just like one leak is sufficient to sink an entire ship. Do not have communion today. Instead, pray, read the Bible and come to church. God hears those who call on him in truth.'

By this time Equiano had been a long time out of work, busy pondering the state of his soul. Needing money, he signed up for a ship bound for Spain. Yet as soon as he went aboard, he was certain he'd made the wrong decision. *The sailors swear all the time. I have heard the gospel now, and have no excuse. Surely if I swear just once more, even accidentally, I will be condemned forever.*

Equiano ran to the captain and begged him three times. 'Please, release me from my contract.'

'Vassa,' the captain said each time, 'You are doing good work here. I will pay you extra if you stay.'

Terrified he would go to hell, Equiano spent long hours staring into the ocean and making everyone around him miserable. Finally, as the ship had not yet sailed, he went back on land.

'Vassa,' his Christian friends said, 'you are a good sailor. This is your calling.'

'I can't go on this voyage,' he fretted. 'I can't.'

'You've signed up already,' they encouraged him. 'It's your duty.' One of them read Hebrews 11 and prayed with Equiano until he felt a bit more peaceful.

'Alright,' he said, reboarding the ship. 'Let whatever God wills, happen.'

The ship left for Spain, and Equiano spent all his free hours reading his Bible and praying, still struggling to find assurance.

On 6th October, 1774, Equiano got up from his hammock feeling on edge. All day he felt as though something big was about to happen, and thinking he was going to die, he begged God constantly for help.

That evening, God brought light for Equiano. He saw himself, utterly condemned by the law, a sinner unable to get to heaven. He saw Jesus before him, crucified on the cross, bleeding for his sins. He saw that everything in his life, from his kidnapping as a child, to the obstacles which had prevented him going to Turkey to become a Muslim, had been leading up to this moment.

Equiano wept. Heaven is free, bought by Jesus! At last, at long last, he was certain he would be saved. All his past efforts to do good meant nothing — it was God in his mercy, who had hunted him down and snatched him from judgment.

Crying, and praying for the salvation of his mother and his friends and all the people who did not know his wonderful God, Equiano burst out of his cabin. 'I know the love of Jesus!' he bellowed to the surprised sailors on deck. 'God has been good, so good to me!'

Go to the Nations!

'Will you come with me to Nicaragua?' asked Dr Charles Irving. 'I wish to establish a plantation where people are treated kindly, and I want you to be the overseer.'

Equiano tilted his head to one side. Ever since he had seen the grace and mercy of God, every voyage had become an opportunity to share the gospel. On a second journey to Spain he'd had many conversations with a Spanish priest, who had tried to convince Equiano that England was living in sin because everyone was allowed to read the Bible for themselves. 'No,' Equiano had said, 'Christ calls us to search the Scriptures.'

He thought of Jamaica and Nicaragua, of the people there who had never heard the good news. *The harvest is ripe. Perhaps God will use me as his instrument.*

'I will go with you,' Equiano told Dr Irving.

'Ah good!' said the Scottish inventor. 'Four Indians will be returning with us. English traders brought them over here, so they could complain on their behalf against the British Government's control of the Mosquito Coast. Now the Government is paying to have them returned.'

Eight days before they left England, Equiano went to speak to the Indians.

'No,' they replied to his questions, 'we were baptised when we came to Britain, but have not been to any church.'

'Has anyone taught you what it means to be a Christian?' Equiano asked, remembering how even at his own baptism he had not truly understood the gospel.

The Indians shook their heads.

'Next Sunday,' Equiano promised, 'I will take you to church. Christianity is not only about being baptised.'

On their November voyage to the Caribbean, Equiano spent all the time he could with the four Indians, one of whom was a prince of his people. If only the prince came to know Jesus, surely all his people would follow!

'Jesus died for Indians?' The prince asked, trying to understand Equiano's faith.

'Yes!' said Equiano, 'for all people.' He prayed constantly for the prince's salvation, and often the prince would join him in his prayers. He taught him the alphabet, and began to teach him how to read.

Yet as the ship neared the Mosquito Coast, the other sailors began to tease the prince. 'Oh you've converted to Christianity, have you?' they laughed. 'Equiano's faith is too gloomy. The devil doesn't exist, there is nothing to fear. Just enjoy yourself!'

The Indian prince turned to Equiano. 'I don't understand,' he said. 'Why do all the white men who are so clever and know all the things of the world, still lie and drink and swear? You are the only one who doesn't do these things.'

'I fear God,' Equiano replied. 'They do not, and will not find happiness with him.'

'Well,' said the prince, 'if these white people go to hell, I will go with them.'

'But that will not make it any less horrible!' protested Equiano. 'It doesn't matter if you have company, if you do not have God.'

Troubled, the prince turned away. For the rest of the voyage he kept away from both Equiano and the white sailors, preferring to be alone. After the ship landed on the coast, Equiano took the prince to a church, but when the Indians came to say their goodbyes to the British, Equiano was not sure if the prince had decided what he believed.

I did my best, Lord. You must work now.

* * *

Dr Irving, Equiano and the African slaves began to set up camp on the coast of Nicaragua. They were soon joined by the Indians who lived nearby and helped them decide on a location for the plantation.

'Here we go!' Dr Irving said. 'This soil is rich, and near the riverbank. We should have a quick crop of vegetables here.'

'And when our ship comes back from trading down the Black River, we'll have all we need for our first season here.' Equiano said.

Each night they lit blazing fires to keep away wild animals, and the doctor cured poisonous snake bites with rum and pepper. The Indians came from all around to the doctor for medical treatment, but refused all offers of employment.

It was a strange land to Equiano, very different to the West Indies plantations he'd worked on. He and the doctor slept in safety, attended parties with the Indians, and tried pineapple rum and dried turtle meat.

Everyday there were new sights to see, or new Indian customs to observe, but soon Equiano began to get disheartened. He had wanted to come to preach the gospel, but surviving in the jungle took all of their time, particularly after their trading vessel was captured by the Spanish.

Day slipped into day, and it was difficult to remember when Sunday was. The Indians were mostly kind and honest people, but uninterested in learning about the Western way of living, or about Equiano's faith. Equiano tried to be a kind and caring overseer to the African slaves, treating them well and making sure their work was light, but he had no time to tell them about Jesus and no other Christians to help him.

'The rain just doesn't stop!' exclaimed Dr Irving. The wet season had begun, and with it came tremendous rains. Soon all the food they had so carefully planted was washed away.

Equiano sighed deeply. *Nothing is going right, Lord. Is this a sign you don't want us here?* Finally, unable to continue to live in a place where he was the only Christian, and was unable to worship on Sundays or share the gospel, Equiano went to Dr Irving.

'I can't stay here any longer,' he said. Reluctantly, and only after Equiano had listed his many reasons, the doctor agreed to let him return to Jamaica, and then England.

* * *

'You will work on that boat, or I will force you to work as a slave!' the owner of the ship raged.

'But I do not want to go on that boat,' Equiano protested. 'You promised me a passage to Jamaica – you have no right to try and send me onto another ship! If you won't take me, put me ashore.'

The owner swore. 'Unless you can use your Christian faith to walk on the water like the apostle Peter, you won't be going ashore. I'll sell you in Spain!'

'What right do you have to sell me?'

The owner turned away from Equiano and shouted at his slaves. 'Tie him up and hang him from the mast!' The slaves refused, so the captain beat them and then called to his sailors. 'You do it!'

Unable to protect himself against so many men, Equiano was soon suspended in the air and left hanging.

'Please!' he cried, pain shooting through his arms and legs. 'Cut me down. Have mercy!'

'Stop wailing, or I'll shoot you,' growled the owner, and went to bed.

Equiano fell silent. What could he do? The law would not defend him. All the white men aboard ignored him. At one in the morning, when all was quiet on deck, he called out to one of the black slaves.

'Please, I am in so much pain. Will you loosen the ropes a bit so at least my feet can rest against the deck?' The slave, risking another beating, did so.

At 6 o'clock in the morning, the owner woke and, realising he couldn't hoist the ships sails because Equiano was in the way, cut him down. Equiano at once found a sympathetic sailor and convinced him to speak to the captain on his behalf. The captain let him go.

As Equiano rowed his canoe to shore, the owner of the ship, realising what had happened, began shooting at him! Splash — splash — splash — every one of the bullets missed. 'Thank you Lord for delivering me yet again!' cried Equiano when he at last stumbled ashore.

To Equiano's disappointment, two more ships pretended they were going to Jamaica, and then, once he was aboard, forced him to work for them, using threats and violence. One captain threatened to blow the entire ship up with Equiano on it! Again and again God worked amazing acts of deliverance for Equiano, and sustained him during his sufferings.

Finally, at the beginning of 1777, Equiano arrived in England. I've had enough of life at sea for now, he decided.

* * *

'Have you ever thought of returning to Africa as a missionary?' Equiano's employer asked.

'No,' Equiano replied. 'All my attempts at spreading the gospel overseas have ended in disaster. Even when the Indian prince seemed interested, the white men on board sowed so much doubt in his mind that he gave up praying with me.'

'But I could write to the Bishop of London,' his employer said. 'You could be ordained as a missionary, and supported by a church.'

Equiano thought hard. He'd received news that all the African slaves he'd cared for with Dr Irving had been drowned trying to escape the cruelty of the white overseer who had taken Equiano's place. *God, I want to do good for my people!* 'Let's try,' he told his employer.

Their letters were met with one answer: No. The Church of England had sent an African missionary to Africa before, but the results had been unpromising. They did not wish to send another.

* * *

'Have you heard about the Zong massacre?' Equiano demanded, the moment he entered Granville Sharp's drawing room.

The abolitionist shook his head. He was always looking for a way to bring slavery before the courts. 'Tell me more.'

'Two years ago,' Equiano began, 'The *Zong*, a slave ship on its way to Jamaica, threw 130 Africans into the ocean, alive. They all drowned. The crew claimed it was because they were low on water.'

'That's terrible —'

Equiano held up a hand. 'Yes, but what's worse is that when the ship arrived in Jamaica, the owners put in an insurance claim for the people they murdered.' He stood up and began to pace, agitated. 'The insurers refused, and the owners took them to court. The jury has just made a decision.'

'What did they decide?'

'That in some cases, the murder of Africans is legal, the crew are not at fault, and the insurers must pay for the loss of property.'

'That's preposterous!' Granville Sharp stood up and joined his friend in pacing the room. 'I will take them back to court,' he promised, 'and have them prosecuted for murder.'

* * *

'Have you heard about the Government's latest project?'

It was 1786, and Equiano, having just returned to British soil after his latest sea voyage, shook his head.

'They are looking for a solution to all the ex-slaves who have ended up in London after the American civil war,' his friend replied. 'They've decided to sponsor the establishment of an African settlement in Sierra Leone. Any of the black poor can volunteer to be re-settled. They want you to go!'

'What do you think?' Equiano asked his friend. Like him, Ottobah Cugoano was a freed African slave, a strong Christian who'd managed to obtain an education and reputation among people of influence. He too had worked with Granville Sharp to try and bring the issue of slavery before the law courts.

Cugoano sighed, leaning back in his chair. 'It feels too rushed. The Government has not spoken to the inhabitants of Sierra Leone. Besides, our people are frightened that it's a trap, and they will be sold or kidnapped back into slavery the moment they set foot in Africa. And why shouldn't they be? The Government allows the slave trade on one hand and then promises to pay for a free settlement on the other!'

Equiano and Cugoano were two of only a handful of educated black men in London. The vast majority had never been given the chance to learn to read, write or engage in business. While committees, run by donations, had been set up to provide food and employment for the 'black poor', it had soon become clear that a solution other than hand-outs was required.

Yet the fears surrounding the proposed settlement made sense. A large proportion of England's black population had never even been to Africa, and only a few years before Africa had been considered as a potential place to send prisoners. Indeed, the Sierra Leone project was being prepared alongside the First Fleet which would take convicts to Australia – the ships would even sail part of the way together. Newspapers frequently compared the two expeditions, and many readers assumed they were connected. No wonder rumours were spreading that Britain was actually sending their black population to Botany Bay!

'I'll see what the people in charge have to say,' Equiano told his friend.

* * *

'We want to create a free, black settlement on the African coast.' The men in the committee told Equiano. 'We want you to oversee the project and go with the settlers to Africa.'

'But what about slave traders?' Equiano asked. 'I won't take people to Sierra Leone just to be recaptured. The slave trade has not been condemned by the Government. Why should this little settlement be exempt?'

'This is a government sponsored project,' the committee replied. 'You will travel on Royal Navy ships, and be supported financially for the first three months. In fact, the ships are already in the harbour. One hundred and thirty people have volunteered.'

One hundred and thirty was not very many out of the entire black population. Still, thought Equiano, perhaps I may do good for my people in this situation. He imagined a free, black community in Africa where Christ's love could be taught faithfully every Sunday and smiled. The gospel might even travel into the rest of the country!

'I'll join,' he told the committee.

So, in November 1786, Equiano became 'Commissary of Provisions and Stores for the Black Poor to Sierra

Leone', and headed down to the docks where the ships bound for Sierra Leone were waiting. As the Government continued to recruit volunteers, eventually deciding that aid would only be paid to the poor who agreed to resettle, Equiano did his best to prepare for the voyage.

'Where are the rest of the clothes?' Equiano asked the agent, frustrated. 'I am to prepare for 750 people, but I can't find more than 426 sets!'

The agent shrugged. 'They haven't been bought.'

'Haven't been bought? But the Government has paid for them. Where did the money go?'

The agent shrugged again.

Equiano frowned. *Someone is mismanaging or stealing government funds. But more importantly, they are stealing from the poor volunteers!*

Soon voices were coming from all directions, and Equiano stood in the stormy centre, employed by the white men but seen by the black settlers as their spokesman. There were now about 400 volunteers out of the hoped for 750, but numbers had become the least of the Government's problems.

'Equiano,' came the voices of the black settlers. 'There are not enough beds on board, and there are not enough clothes for all of us. Water is running out.'

Having been aboard the ships, Equiano knew that what they said was true. Conditions were awful, several people had died, and with their memories of previous slave voyages, the settlers were beginning to get anxious.

'The settlers are undisciplined and disruptive!' complained the ships' captains to the Government. 'We need to set sail immediately, before the situation gets worse.'

'A sickness is spreading through the ships,' worried the Government. 'We need to get new clothes for everyone to prevent infection.'

'The agent Joseph Irwin is taking money and supplies, and not passing them on to the settlers,' Equiano informed the treasury. 'Where is the bedding and the clothes? Where is the sugar and the tea and other provisions the Government has paid for? The women and children are suffering.'

'Equiano is encouraging the settlers to mutiny,' Irwin complained to the Government.

'Equiano is trying to ruin the peace,' said one captain, 'but Irwin isn't being helpful either!'

At last the Government dismissed Equiano from his position, the ships sailed, and the newspapers erupted in a flurry of criticism against Equiano, the project, and the Government.

Equiano also got out his pen. 'I did not know why I was dismissed,' he wrote to the Treasury, 'it seems that by trying to ensure justice I have made powerful enemies.'

When the Treasury paid him for his work several months later, Equiano accepted it as a recognition of his faithfulness. The Sierra Leone project had meant well, he thought, and the Government did their best.

It was the mismanagement of funds which was the main problem.

The project, even without Equiano, was not a success. After four years, only 60 of the 375 settlers were still alive.

'No wonder,' Equiano wrote. 'They were cooped up in ships from October to June before they sailed, and were worn out before they even arrived.' Yet the failed project left Equiano with a burning question.

How would God make him useful to his people?

He will Speak with a Loud Voice

'You did well to publish your thoughts,' Equiano told Ottobah Cugoano, holding a copy of his friend's book, *Thoughts and Sentiments on the Evil and Wicked Traffic of the Slavery and Commerce of the Human Species*. 'If we will not speak for our people, who will?' Equiano waved his pen. 'I am writing a petition to Queen Charlotte.'

'Good idea,' said Cugoano. 'It's no use writing to King George III, but maybe his wife will be able to get him to change his pro-slavery views.'

'I do not,' Equiano wrote, 'want pity for my own sufferings. Rather, I ask for your compassion for millions of my African countrymen, who groan under the lash of tyranny in the West Indies.'

The other literate Africans in London were also picking up their pens. After the very public Sierra Leone affair; the recent publication of Thomas Clarkson's popular anti-slavery essay; and the formation of a Committee for the Abolition of the African Slave Trade, the newspapers were exploding with letters about slavery.

'We are … greatly indebted to you,' Equiano and eleven other Africans wrote to Granville Sharp in 1787, 'for your many good services to us. May the blessing and peace of the Almighty God be with you.'

Calling themselves the Sons of Africa, Equiano and the eleven filled the newspapers with letters of thanks to prominent white abolitionists, as well as book reviews and descriptions of slavery. Often ending their letters with the line, 'For ourselves and our Brethren', they were determined to keep the horrors of slavery in front of the public, and are thought to be Britain's first black political organisation.

Equiano personally replied to many unfair and racist letters by slavery supporters, determined to prove that all people were equal, regardless of the colour of their skin. Yet as he did so, he was busy working on an even greater project.

* * *

'I am going to write a book,' Equiano told his friends one evening.

It was something he'd been thinking deeply about. Out of the ten thousand people of African origin in London, only a dozen were able to pick up pens and write. Furthermore, compared to the millions of Africans kidnapped from their homeland, God had placed him in a unique situation. Time and time again, he'd been given the opportunity to continue his education, obtain his freedom, and gain a standing in the eyes of the British population.

His extensive travels also meant that he could stand as a witness to African suffering across the continents and in many different contexts. Most slaves lived and died toiling on faraway plantations, seen and heard by no one except God in heaven. Equiano had been favoured and fortunate, and now, he decided, he would speak out with a loud voice for the good of his people.

'I might say,' he began, writing in his London room in 1788, 'my sufferings were great: but when I compare my lot with that of most of my countrymen, I regard myself as a particular favourite of Heaven, and acknowledge the mercies of Providence in every occurrence of my life.'

Equiano wrote and wrote. He looked up statistics and books about slavery until his desk was overflowing with papers. He spoke to other Africans about their experiences, and copied out in full his precious references and manumission papers, determined to prove that his character was sound, and his voice worth listening to.

Most of all, he reflected on the many ways God had delivered him time and time again, nudging him towards the cross, and equipping him to be a witness for Africa. He thought of the occasion he'd heard George Whitefield speak in Philadelphia, and how impressed he'd been at his passion, even before he'd become a Christian.

'Yet on, dejected, still I went –
Heart-throbbing woes within were pent;
Nor land, nor sea, could comfort give,
Nothing my anxious mind relieve.'

Equiano composed a poem, remembering his terrible doubts and fear of eternity.

'... [Then] light came in, and I believed;
Myself forgot, and help received!
My saviour then I know I found,
For, eased from guilt, no more I groaned.'

He recalled a visit to the American colonies, when a black slave had convinced him to perform a Christian burial for her dead child, because every white minister had refused.

'I'm not a minister,' Equiano had protested.

'There's no one else!' the woman had wept.

He thought of men who kept their half African children as slaves on their plantations in the West Indies, and were allowed to murder them for the price of fifteen pounds.

'Oh ye nominal Christians!' Equiano wrote, 'if these are not the poor, the broken-hearted, the blind, the captive, the bruised, which our Saviour speaks of, who are they?'

* * *

At last the book was finished.

'I've titled it, *The Interesting Narrative of The Life of Olaudah Equiano, or Gustavus Vassa, The African*. Written by himself,' he said. He certainly had become a man of many names and, in using them all, he would remind people of both his African and British identities.

'Who will you get to publish it?' asked Cugoano, rifling through the 530 loose pages. 'The Quakers will certainly help. They have published many pamphlets promoting abolition.'

'I'm going to raise the money by selling advanced copies,' Equiano interrupted. 'This is my story, and although I don't own much in the world, I want to own my words.'

And so, when his book came out in 1789, Equiano, now in his late-forties, worked tirelessly to promote it. He chose bookshops in strategic places to stock copies, and made sure each time a prominent person subscribed, everyone heard of the endorsement. He commissioned an artist and printed a painting of himself on the inside cover, holding a Bible open to Acts 4:12: 'Salvation is found in no one else, for there is no other name under heaven given to mankind by which we must be saved.' He even sent copies to the Members of Parliament with a letter explaining that he wished to 'excite a sense of compassion for the miseries which the slave trade has brought on my unfortunate countrymen.'

His friends and colleagues, congratulating him on his work, wrote letters of introduction so he could travel and promote the book all across Britain.

'I take the liberty of introducing to your notice Gustavus Vassa,' wrote abolitionist Thomas Clarkson to those in Cambridge, 'a very honest, ingenious, and industrious African.'

It was a good thing Thomas did take 'the liberty' of introducing him, because on his journey to

Cambridgeshire, Equiano met someone very important – his future wife!

Susannah Cullen of Ely was an English woman of Scottish descent who had previously been one of Equiano's subscribers. The two, both strong Christians, were married on 7 April, 1792, in St Andrews church, Soham, Cambridgeshire.

As Equiano led his wife through the crowds after the service, he couldn't help but remember something he'd seen in the West Indies long ago.

'I'm glad we're in England,' he said. 'So we don't have to be married in a boat!'

'Me too!' Susannah replied, clutching his arm. She remembered the passage in her new husband's book, which described a wedding between a white man and a free black woman in the West Indies. The engaged pair had to be married on a small boat in the harbour to avoid the law against mixed-race marriages on land! 'I'm also looking forward to our travels through Scotland.'

'Yes,' Equiano said, almost unable to take his eyes off his bride. 'It will be nice not to have to travel alone on this book tour!'

That year Equiano published the fifth edition of his book in Edinburgh. It was a bestseller, and he would publish nine editions in total. His story of slavery and salvation reached thousands of hands and touched thousands of hearts.

Many paid attention to his prayer that, 'If [those who are privileged], when they look round the world, feel exultation, let it be tempered with benevolence to others, and gratitude to God, "who has made of one blood all nations of men to dwell on the face of the earth.'"

It was a tumultuous time. Thomas Paine published his ground-breaking book *Rights of Man*, the French Revolution was in full swing, and people everywhere were boycotting sugar and signing petitions against slavery. Wilberforce gave speeches in Parliament; Thomas Clarkson was collecting testimonies against the slave trade; and everyone, it seemed, was reading Equiano's book.

'We want rights!' Thomas Hardy, part of the radical London Corresponding Society, shouted, slamming his hand on the table, 'For black and poor alike!'

Equiano, who had updated his memoir while staying in Hardy's house, heartily agreed.

Then everything changed.

'France has declared war!' The news spread. 'The Government is afraid of an English revolution! No large gatherings are permitted.'

Thomas Hardy was arrested and the parliamentary action against the slave trade was suspended, yet Equiano continued steadfastly promoting and selling his book. Slowly but surely, the British opinion of slavery began to change for the better. As his two daughters, Maria and Joanna were born, Equiano heard news that his memoir had been pirated, translated, and was now for sale in the Netherlands, New York, Russia and Germany. While this was illegal, it did mean that 'The African' was being heard!

In 1796, however, tragedy struck Equiano's life. After a long illness, his wife Susannah died. She was only thirty-four, and knowing she was going to die, wrote, '[I commit my] soul into the hands of the Almighty God in whom and by whose mercy I trust.'

Equiano did not have much time to grieve before he too fell ill. One of the very few Africans in the eighteenth century who had enough money to even write a will, he left his hard-earned fortune to his daughters.

Granville Sharp came to visit his friend on his deathbed, but Equiano, who had spoken so eloquently for so long, barely had the energy to whisper. He died on 31st March 1797, not yet sixty, but thoroughly certain of his eternal future. The boy who had been ripped from his homeland and denied every protection of the law because of the colour of his skin, was Home at last and had a freedom no one could ever take away.

His eldest daughter died soon after, and only Joanna Vassa lived to witness the abolition of the African slave trade ten years later, and the abolition of slavery itself twenty-six years after that.

So well known while he was alive and so pivotal in the fight for abolition, Equiano's voice lay unheard for decades, until his memoir re-gained popularity for a time during the American civil rights movement, and again more recently as historians seek to uncover the stories of the 12.5 million Africans displaced by the slave trade.

For Equiano, the powerful story of God working in his life was only important if those who heard it were changed. '…After all, what makes any event important,' he wrote on the final page of his memoir, quoting Micah 6:8, 'unless by its observation we become better and wiser, and learn "to do justly, to love mercy, and to walk humbly before God"?'

Olaudah Equiano
Timeline

1745 (or, more likely, 1742) – Olaudah Equiano is born in Essaka, Benin (Nigeria).

1753 Equiano is kidnapped at age eleven, along with his sister.

1754 Middle Passage: Equiano is taken from the Bight of Biafra in Africa to Barbados (West Indies) and then to Virginia where he is bought by a tobacco planter. He is sold shortly afterwards to British naval officer Michael Henry Pascal, captain of *Industrious Bee*. Taken to England.

1756 -63
Seven Years War. Equiano serves in the Royal Navy as Pascal's servant. He is involved in the Battle of Louisbourg (Canada).

1759 Baptised at St Margaret's Church, London. Godparents are the Guerins, cousins of Pascal.

1760 King George III becomes king.

1762 Equiano is promoted to rank of able seaman; denied freedom. Sold to James Doran, captain of the *Charming Sally*.

1763 Equiano is sold to Robert King in Montserrat (West Indies).

1766 Equiano purchases his freedom. Works for King aboard the *Nancy*.

1767 Equiano is shipwrecked in the Bahamas; returns to London; trains as a hairdresser and continues education.

1768 Equiano returns to sea and travels the Mediterranean.

1773 Equiano goes on the Arctic expedition aboard *HMS Racehorse* as Dr Charles Irving's assistant

1774 Equiano experiences a spiritual rebirth.

1775 Equiano returns to the West Indies in the hope of sharing his new faith on the Mosquito Shore (Nicaragua). The venture fails.

1779 Equiano seeks appointment as a missionary to Africa from the Lord Bishop of London. He is turned down.

1783 Equiano informs abolitionist Granville Sharp of the *Zong* massacre.

1786 Equiano is appointed Commissary of Provisions and Stores for the Black Poor to Sierra Leone. Becomes increasingly frustrated at the misuse of funds and poor management which results in much suffering for the black settlers.

1787 Equiano is dismissed as Commissary and attacked in the press. The Sierra Leone Expedition proves to be a failure, but Equiano emerges as a public figure. He becomes involved in writing letters to the newspaper against slavery, as part of 'Sons of Africa'.

The Society for Effecting the Abolition of the Slave Trade is formed; Thomas Clarkson begins to collect evidence and William Wilberforce agrees to take the matter to parliament.

1788 Equiano presents a petition to Queen Charlotte against the slave trade.

1789 *The Interesting Narrative of the life of Olaudah Equiano, or Gustavus Vassa, the African* is published. Equiano begins touring and promotion across Britain. Thomas Clarkson writes him a letter of introduction to Cambridge, where Equiano meets Susannah Cullen.

The French Revolution begins.

1792 Equiano marries Susannah Cullen of Ely, Cambridgeshire. They have two daughters, only one of which survives infancy.

1793 Britain goes to war against France.

1796 Susannah dies.

1797 Equiano dies in London, 31 March. His eldest daughter dies four months later.

1807 Abolition of the slave trade.

1833 Abolition of slavery.

Thinking Further Topics

Chapter 1: The Fortunate One

Olaudah Equiano's people believed that their god gave everyone a special purpose in life. As Christians we also believe that God has a plan for each of our lives, even if we don't yet know what the future will look like. To find out more about God's plan for you, look up: Ephesians 1:4-5; Ephesians 2:10; Romans 8:28-29.

Chapter 2: Kidnapped!

After being kidnapped from his village, Olaudah discovers that a slave never really has a place to call home. The Bible tells us that Christians also do not have real homes on earth – but for a very different reason! Our true home is in heaven with God. (Hebrews 11:13-16; John 14:2) We can enjoy our earthly homes, knowing that there is a better home coming. Have you ever had to leave your earthly home? How might it help you to know that no one can ever take your heavenly home away?

Chapter 3: In a World of Angry Spirits

Have you ever felt like you are more important than your friends? Or do you ever feel less important? Why? On board the slave ship, Equiano is treated very badly because the white slavers believe that he is less important than them. Yet God tells us that he loves all people the same, and everyone is equally important in his eyes (Acts 10:34-35; Galatians 3:28). How might this truth change the way you treat your friends today? (Matthew 25:37-40; John 15:12-13)

Chapter 4: Becoming Gustavus Vassa

Equiano believes there are gods which control the sea and weather, and he is very afraid of them. Yet when he hears about the true God, he is interested and wants to hear more. What do you know about God which makes you want to know him better? (If you need some ideas, read Psalm 145, and highlight every word used to describe God). Who really controls the ocean? (Mark 4:35-41)

Chapter 5: At War!

Have you been baptised? When Equiano is baptised he thinks that makes him a Christian as long as he also does good. Is this true? (Romans 3:23; Galatians 3:11) What really makes someone a Christian? (John 3:16; Acts 16:31; Ephesians 2:8-9) Have you ever tried to make God love you by doing good things like going to church? Why doesn't this work? (John 14:6; Hebrews 11:6)

Chapter 6: Back to the West Indies

Equiano meets a slave who believes that God is his only chance for justice. When Equiano and the slave wait outside the door of the men who stole their fruit, they eventually receive some back. This is similar to the

Parable of the Persistent Widow in Luke 18:1-8. Have you ever been treated unfairly? Is it helpful to know that God loves to be just and to treat people fairly? (Psalm 140:12; Isaiah 30:18) Why?

Chapter 7: Forty Pounds for a Life

Equiano has many dreams, and believes God is talking to him through them. The Bible tells us that God can speak through dreams, although we don't know for sure if he was doing so here. (1 Kings 3:5; Mathew 2:19) What does the Bible say to do if we have a dream we think might be from God? (James 1:5; Hebrews 4:12; 1 John 4:1-3) Even without dreams we know that God calls us to love those around us, just as Equiano did when he saved the ship from being wrecked (Matthew 22:39). How can you love someone near you today?

Chapter 8: Knocking at the Door

Equiano wants to know for certain if he's saved. He feels he's not good enough to get into heaven. If Equiano was telling you his fears, what would you say to him? (2 Corinthians 5:21; 1 John 1:9; Luke 11:9-10). It's a wonderful thing to be able to know that you are saved and going to live with Jesus one day. Are you certain of this?

Chapter 9: Go to the Nations!

Equiano doesn't give up, even when the Mosquito Coast plantation and the Sierra Leone Project seem to have failed – why do you think this is? (Luke 2:10; Romans 10:14-15) What does God call all believers to do, once they've heard the gospel? (Matthew 28:16-20) Who can you tell about Jesus? Pray now for an opportunity to tell them why you love Jesus.

Chapter 10: He will Speak with a Loud Voice

God chose to fulfil the prophecy made at Equiano's birth – in publishing his book, Equiano really did get to 'speak with a loud voice'! Words and stories have great power. The Bible is the story of God and has the power to change lives, just as it changed Equiano's (2 Timothy 3:16; Romans 1:16; 1 Thessalonians 2:13). Who could you write a letter to? Perhaps you can tell them a bit about Equiano, and how God worked in his life! Don't forget to write about how God has changed your life too.

APPENDIX

A Man of Many Names

In this biography I have chosen to call Olaudah Equiano by his African birth name. This was not such an easy decision. Equiano was a man of many names. While named 'the fortunate one' on African soil, he was called 'Michael' during the Middle Passage and 'Jacob' when toiling in Virginia. The Navy lieutenant Michael Pascal ironically re-christened him 'Gustavus Vassa', the name of a Swedish freedom-fighter.

Although he fought the designation at the time, Equiano would go on to embrace it, and was known as Gustavus Vassa until his death in 1797. It was the name on his baptismal record, his manumission papers and his wedding certificate. His wife and children had the last name 'Vassa' and indeed, one of his fellow abolitionists noted that he did not like being called 'Olaudah Equiano'. In fact, he only seems to use his birth name as a complement to 'Gustavus Vassa' when he wished to emphasise his African heritage, such as in his pro-abolition newspaper letters, and memoir.

Perhaps Vassa wished to protect the sacredness of his original name, or perhaps he wanted to stress that his very identity had been destroyed by the slave trade, and he was no longer the free son of an African elder. Perhaps 'Gustavus Vassa' was an important link to his Christian identity, being his baptismal name, or perhaps he was simply tired of being called by multiple names! We will never know.

In the intervening years however, it has become common practice for scholars and historians to refer to Equiano by his African name, and to avoid confusion I have also chosen to do so. It is important to note that 'Equiano' was not his surname in the way 'Vassa' is, but simply the second half of his full name: Olaudah Equiano.

A Controversial Man

In recent years the story of Olaudah Equiano, as told in his memoir T*he Interesting Narrative of the Life of Olaudah Equiano, or Gustavus Vassa the African* (1789), has come under some scrutiny. Scholar Vincent Carretta in his 2005 book, *Equiano, the African: Biography of a Self-made Man*, has suggested that Olaudah Equiano was not born in Africa, but rather South Carolina, U.S.A. The basis for Carretta's assertion is Olaudah's baptismal record, entered in the parish record of St Margaret on 9th February 1759: 'Gustavus Vassa a Black born in Carolina 12 years old,' and an entry on the *Racehorse* muster list for the Arctic expedition of 1773, which lists a 'Gustavus Weston', a seaman, aged twenty-eight and born in South Carolina. While these two documents mean that scholars must admit that there is uncertainty surrounding the early part of Equiano's narrative, there are several good reasons for believing that Equiano's African origins, as told in his own words, remain true.

Firstly, while Equiano most certainly wrote his memoirs in order to fill a need – that of a black witness against slavery – it is for this reason that he had every motivation to tell the truth. At the time of his writing the opponents of abolition were trying to smear the reputations of those fighting slavery. The likelihood of personal defamation and the damage to the abolitionist cause would simply have been too high for Equiano to risk altering his birth story. Indeed in 1792, abolition opponents did accuse Equiano of manufacturing his African origins. Apparently unaware of both his baptismal register and the muster list mentioned above, they falsely claimed he had been born on the Danish island of Santa Cruz [St Croix], in the West Indies – a claim Equiano denied in a subsequent edition of his memoir.

It's also important to note that the fabrication of his birth is inconsistent with the narrative as a whole. The fact is, that when it can be checked against external sources, his memoir is surprisingly accurate. The few exceptions are the dates which he proposes he left Africa and arrived in England. This makes sense, given that Equiano was a young, traumatised child at the time. Given that the dates of the ships' arrival are on record and could have been checked, either Equiano did very bad research for his fake birth story, or he was actually relying on his imperfect childhood memory.

Furthermore, Equiano mentions that he is circumcised several times in his memoir, an observation which plays little part in the narrative as a whole, and could easily have been left out. Circumcision was widely practised in Africa, and was not practised among African-American slaves. Equiano's wife, at the very least, would have known whether he was telling the truth, and indeed, the mark of his circumcision was certainly a sign which he could have used to prove his veracity, had such a need arisen.

Why then, are there two records which name 'Carolina' as Equiano's birthplace? It has been suggested that Equiano knowingly provided erroneous information as a child, wanting to re-create his past and forget his African birth. This is possible, although seems unlikely, considering Equiano's consistent emphasis on telling the truth within his narrative, and is out of line with his spiritual belief at the time, that he had to keep the Ten Commandments in order to avoid damnation. If the information was provided by either his godparents or master, it could easily have been a misunderstanding – Equiano had, after all, been bought from America, or it could have been a wilful obscuring of the truth due to the tentative place of African slavery in the British Navy. By the time the muster roll for the *Racehorse* was recorded, Equiano was a free man. Yet, his place in society, as the narrative suggests, was still precarious. It is quite possible that Equiano felt unable to contradict his baptismal record.

A final important point to take into account is Equiano's Christian beliefs. They are in fact central throughout the narrative, particularly in the latter half, where he emphasises that even though he did his very best to keep all the commandments, it was not until he understood grace that he felt assured of his salvation. A man so concerned with upright living; a man who explicitly states that God had used his African kidnapping and consequent slavery for the good of his soul, and the good of many, is not a man who would manufacture his birth country. Those who claim that Olaudah lied, place not only Equiano's identity as an African in jeopardy, but also his identity as a Christian.

A Note on Dating

In his memoir Equiano states with a surprising amount of certainty that he was born in 1745 and kidnapped at age eleven. Given that the Igbo counted the years but used a different calendar, his conception of his age when he was kidnapped makes sense. His assurance regarding his birth year is unusual, unless we take into account that American slave-owners had to discover the age of their slaves in order to pay the correct tax. If Equiano was examined at the time of his purchase in Virginia and told his birth year, this both explains his certainty and allows the date to be flexible.

Problems have arisen with the discovery of a baptismal register which states that Equiano was twelve when he was baptised. If this is the case, he must have been born in 1747.

On the contrary, ship records attest to a series of journeys in the year 1754 which fit neatly to Equiano's travels from Africa to West Indies to America to England. However, he would have to have been born in 1742 in order to be eleven when he was kidnapped.

Both these dates are possible due to the necessary flexibility of a 1745 birthdate. Due to shipping data, an African birth in 1742 followed by a kidnapping eleven years later is far easier to account for. A 1747 South Carolinian birth does not explain how Equiano arrived in Virginia eight years later, where he was bought by Pascal.

Overview: Olaudah Equiano (or, Gustavus Vassa) (1745-1797)

Olaudah Equiano, the son of a respected Igbo elder, was born in Essaka, in the kingdom of Benin (probably modern day Nigeria). He was one of seven children, and his name means 'fortunate one' and 'well-spoken'. The priests in his village believed he would be very lucky, yet when he was eleven years-old, Equiano was kidnapped by African slave traders. Although his African masters were kind, Equiano learned that as a slave he could not make decisions and had no control over his life. Before he could escape and return to his village, Equiano was sold to white slave traders.

He was packed onto a ship with many other Africans from all over Africa, and brought across the ocean to the island of Barbados. During the eighteenth century alone over six million Africans were taken from their country in this way to slave on plantations in America and the West Indies. The journey was called the Middle Passage and many perished before reaching land, due to bad treatment and terrible conditions.

From Barbados, Equiano was taken to a plantation in Virginia. There he was bought by a British Naval officer, Michael Pascal. Equiano served Pascal on board many ships during the Seven Years War, and learned how to be a sailor. He also learned about God and was baptised in London. After six years, Equiano believed that Pascal would free him, because slavery was usually not recognised in England. Instead, he was sold to a merchant in the West Indies and was forced to work trading goods and slaves for his new master. When at last he was allowed to purchase his freedom, Equiano made his way back to England.

There he worked hard as a servant and a sailor to earn money and obtain an education. He became a hair-dresser, learnt the French horn, and even went on an expedition to the Arctic! As he worked, he did his very best to be a 'good' Christian but soon became frustrated with his inability to keep all the commandments. In 1774 he had a vision, and realised, once and for all, that it was Jesus' blood which had saved him, not his own works.

After the American civil war, London became home to many ex-slaves. Upon returning from a failed attempt to create a 'humane' slave plantation in the West Indies, Equiano was appointed as a Commissary for the Sierra Leone Project, which sought to return some of these refugees to Africa. Yet after uncovering a misuse of funds and doing his best to intercede for his countrymen, Equiano was dismissed. Along with other Africans in London he began to write letters to the newspapers against slavery, and personally sent a petition to Queen Charlotte.

Finally Equiano realised that telling his own story of slavery would help convince people slavery was wrong. He called his 1789 book: *The Interesting Narrative of the Life of Olaudah Equiano, or Gustavus Vassa, the African* and published nine editions. For six years he travelled around the U.K. selling copies and speaking about abolition. During this time he married a British woman, Susannah Cullen and they had two children. Sadly, within four years, Equiano, his wife and his oldest child all caught an illness and died. Although he did not live to see the end of slavery, Equiano's book played an important role. It is not only a gripping story of slavery and freedom, but also a powerful testimony of God working through horrific circumstance to bring about great good.

Modern Day Slavery

Although African Slavery was abolished in Britain in 1833, slavery still exists in many forms today. In some countries poor parents are forced to sell their children or themselves into slavery in order to buy food or pay off a debt. In other countries, young women are promised safe passage and a new life in another place, only to find themselves held captive and forced to do terrible jobs. Companies which refuse to pay their workers fair wages or give them good working conditions also practise slavery. It is estimated that in 2020 there are over 40 million slaves all over the world, and one in four are children!

The fight against slavery is not over, but take heart. We are not fighting this great evil in our own strength, but are joining in the work of our Saviour, who came to 'proclaim freedom for the prisoners' and 'to set the oppressed free.' (Luke 4:18)

For more stories of modern day slavery, see: https://www.ijm.org/slavery

For a list of organisations working to combat slavery and what you can do to help, see: http://www.endslaverynow.org/connect

Thomas Clarkson
The Giant with One Idea
Emily J. Maurits

Thomas Clarkson was the son of a clergyman who lived in a time when it was legal to buy and sell slaves. He believed this was wrong, and campaigned to make sure this changed. He was instrumental in making sure that no human being could be bought or sold in the British Empire.

Emily J. Maurits
Emily J. Maurits is an Australian blogger and writer. She is the author of the memoir 'Two Sisters and a Brain Tumour' and the founder of Called to Watch, a website supporting those whose loved ones have chronic illnesses.

ISBN: 978-1-5271-0677-2

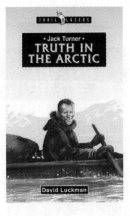

Jack Turner

Truth in the Arctic

David Luckman

Jack Turner was a trained pharmacist and pastor who went to the Arctic to translate God's Word into the native language. It was a world of snow and hunting and anyone who lived there had to become familiar with the ways of living in the Arctic. Ten weeks out of every year the sun never set and for three months the world was in complete darkness.

The spiritual darkness of the North was being pushed back by the power of the gospel and the Lord Jesus Christ that Jack Turner followed. But danger is around every corner in the wild North – and Jack runs into trouble.

ISBN: 978-1-5271-0792-2

Although she is best known for her time on the mission field in Ecuador, Elisabeth Elliot went on to become a vibrant role model for valiant, godly women all over the world. Follow her journey from the jungles of the Amazon, where she faced the tragic death of her first husband, to the lecture halls and radio shows of the culture wars, where she stood as a strong defender of God's Word.

ISBN: 978-1-5271-0161-6

OTHER BOOKS IN THE
TRAIL BLAZERS SERIES

For a full list of Trail Blazers, please see our website:
www.christianfocus.com
All Trail Blazers are available as e-books

CHRISTIAN FOCUS PUBLICATIONS

Christian Focus | Christian Heritage | CF4K | Mentor

Christian Focus Publications publishes books for adults and children under its four main imprints: Christian Focus, CF4K, Mentor and Christian Heritage. Our books reflect our conviction that God's Word is reliable and Jesus is the way to know him, and live for ever with him.

Our children's publication list covers pre-school to early teens. We also publish personal and family devotional titles, biographies and inspirational stories that children will love.

From pre-school board books to teenage apologetics, we have it covered!

**Find us at our web page:
www.christianfocus.com**

CF4•K
Because you're never too young to know Jesus